Have kids, will travel

THE ART OF BACKPACKING AROUND THE WORLD WITH KIDS

MONIQUE COOMBES

©2021 Monique Coombes

All Rights Reserved.

This book is subject to international copyright law. No part may be reproduced by any means without written permission. Inquiries should be made to the author.

ISBN 978-1-925049-34-3

Contents

Acknowledgments	07
The Wanderlust	09
Introduction	11
Turkey	19
Yugoslavia	25
The Aegean Islands	29
Israel	33
Tunisia	37
Mexico	41
New York, Boston and Niagara Falls	47
Andalucia, Southern Spain	49
Morocco	55
Turkey: Cappadocia and the Black Sea	59
Brittany and Normandy	65
The USA	69
Italy: Firenze to South of Rome	75
Corsica	81
The Peloponnese, Greece	85
Dordogne, France	91
Taiwan	95
Hong Kong	103
Puglia, Italy	105
Sardinia	109
Long Weekend in Dubai	113
Australia	117
New Zealand	127
Broken Hill and the Outback	135
Cairns and the Atherton Tablelands	139
Sydney to Adelaide	147
Bangkok and Ayutthaya	153
Northern Italy	157
Berlin, Dresden and Prague	161
New York and Boston	165
Central France and South of France	171
Vanuatu	175
North America	183
Darwin and the Northern Territory	191
Rockhampton and the Capricorn Coast	197
Vietnam / Cambodia	201
China	209
Perth and Western Australia	219
Kuala Lumpur and Penang, Malaysia	223
Sarawak, Borneo	229
Conclusion	237

Acknowledgements

I wish to thank family and friends for the support they have given me and without whom I might not have carried on with this dream. Special thanks to:

My youngest son Marc who did the first edit of the whole book with a great deal of patience;

My friend from Cuba, Heivet, who took time off her PHD studies to devote to the general technical layout of the book, and did it all with such patience and good humour since my IT knowledge was practically non-existent ;

My editor Robert Holden for his professional editing, his many words of encouragement and his belief in my book. Robert paid extremely careful attention to the most minute details including the spelling of place names and I valued his genuine interest in the book.

The publisher Bev Ryan who also encouraged me to have my book published and took precious time off her work to meet me and talk about my book, and whose advice and network connections were invaluable.

"Profite de ta jeunesse et de ta liberté avant l'arrivée des enfants"

The Wanderlust

**HOW IT ALL STARTED AND A FEELING THAT
NOTHING WOULD ALTER.**

The leaves were crackling under my feet when I started university life back in 1976 in France. As ever, apart from my studies, my heart was set on travelling. I shall always remember my dear mother's words: 'Take advantage of your youth to travel before starting a family': *'Profite de ta jeunesse et de ta liberté avant l'arrivée des enfants'*. My Mum was very keen on travelling herself and I have no doubt inherited her genes. I remember thinking that her words were wise – wisdom was one of her defining features – and no doubt true, but in my mind I was convinced that I would carry on travelling independently even after I started a family. Travelling would always breathe some sense of adventure into a life which could easily be humdrum if one did not spice it up with fresh, exciting adventures in some unknown lands; some hot climes where the dry or humid air was full of promise and discoveries; where the world would open its doors to whomever was ready to step through them. I wanted to get acquainted with other ways of life, respect other traditions and be a citizen of the world.

There was definitely not enough time in life to stop travelling while the children were growing up and besides, I strongly believed (and still do) that children benefit from experiencing other countries and cultures, and that these few yearly weeks of travelling independently among the locals would enrich their lives forever.

Introduction

This book attempts to give some personal advice based on my past experiences travelling with rucksacks and kids. However, as it went on, I realized that this book was really my present to my family as I somehow doubted it would ever be published. It may also be a source of help to my children if they choose to travel later on with their own families. It does not pretend to be sacrosanct in its advice and if it sounds arrogant, know-it-all, and obvious in parts, apologies all round. But surprisingly, sometimes the obvious is totally omitted and, of course, everyone has their ideal which might be the opposite of what I have written here. Everything can and probably should be questioned in life, advice can be followed *au pied de la lettre* (word for word) or put aside according to one's own experiences and tastes. The seeds of this book were sown years ago but have not grown to fruition until now, far away Down Under – but that is another story which I might write about eventually.

Trips to various countries have been chronicled to spice this book up and throughout this narrative an attempt has been made to show the different patterns of care to be followed in individual areas of the world and, of course, at the varying ages of the children concerned. This book is, I shall repeat, by no means the only right way to travel with kids, and it does not claim to be so; however, it is a way which suited us, and I wanted to share it with would-be backpackers and their own kids. I noticed while on many of our trips that there were lots of other couples travelling independently, but that many of our adventurous friends had stopped traipsing around the globe once their offspring were born. This is why I wanted to show that at least one adventure a year was a balm on the possible danger of leading a routine life, and could be done with some careful preparation.

Fortunately, I met a man who would become my husband and who shared my love of adventure, sun, and thirst for travelling. As our family grew in size, we went on travelling in our unusual way – at least it was unusual as soon as babies and young children arrived on the scene, although it had not been when we were single, carefree young people. The children did not alter our travelling ways and indeed allowed for more contact with indigenous populations, as people generally could identify with us more than with single adventure-thirsty young people. They were more trusting and also quite curious about us. However, with our little precious bundles, we had to adjust our style; there were some changes that needed to be made, as well as some adaptations to our routines.

For example, we could not accept any odd accommodation where they would be at risk due to unsafe hygienic conditions, and we had to increase our comfort to a certain extent, which was rather an advantage to be honest. More organisation was required, and there was one serious drawback: travelling costs were much higher due to the multiple airfares and so on, which also limited the number of destinations we could visit. Still, it was certainly cheaper to travel that way than through some dreary package tour – and certainly much more fun. You go as you like, as free as a bird, and leave a place when you have exhausted it or if it does not appeal to you. You see so much more that way. By travelling in such a manner, when you say that you have been to such and such country, you have explored it; crisscrossed it, and have a good knowledge of it – not simply taken a quick excursion a few miles away from your hotel and pool in such and such resort. It can of course be tiring, and you will probably need another holiday to rest from the holiday you have just had; however, this is part and parcel of travelling and something that you have to accept. Nobody said that travelling was not tiring!

A backpacking trip with kids starts weeks, maybe even months, before departure and this makes it all the more exciting. The first piece of advice I would give therefore is to plan ahead, a few months ahead ideally, and start with the normal backpacking plans such as searching the different bucket shops and the Internet (not available when we first started) to ensure the flights are ABTA regulated. This will give you a sense of security as far as the company you have entrusted your money to is concerned. As soon as you know your departure date for sure and obtain a reasonable price, it is best to book the flights as soon as possible as the seats fill up quickly at the cheaper prices. Next, a good option is to write to the tourist office of the country you plan to visit; they will give you all sorts of information about accommodation, public transport, tourist sites, and maps. Finally, it is worth investing in a very good tourist guide; this will save you money and time as well as help minimize disappointments. Study the guide carefully and thoroughly, make yourself an itinerary that gives you enough time without having to rush during your trip (a quite typical and frequent mistake of mine), and remember to be realistic. It is best to see less at a more leisurely pace and leave out places that are just too far away for the amount of time you have. Who knows? You might even come back.

You will want to be sure to arrange all the finances with your bank if you require traveller cheques, and inform your bank that you will be travelling abroad as otherwise it could let you down while in a foreign country for fear of fraud! You should always carry a small bag around your neck or on your belt in which you place your cash without it being too noticeable; this is especially advisable in some of the more dangerous areas of the world.

Of course, it goes without saying that carrying valuables such as expensive jewellery attracts unwanted attention and is asking for trouble. Therefore, buy a good rucksack – which should last for years – and aside from the essentials, put as little inside it as possible as you might have to carry it a long way. You will need to be ruthless: you will not need a ball gown for this type of travelling; a couple of nice smart outfits will do the trick for the odd occasion such as a visit to a casino or an invitation to a formal event (although this is unlikely, especially when travelling with children). Should you require something 'posh' all of a sudden, your best bet is to buy something from a local merchant wherever you happen to be; chances are that it will be cheaper, original, and quite unique!

Make sure before departure that the political situation in the country where you intend to travel is safe and stable, and follow the news closely; the world is a cauldron of unease at present. Having said that, do not be too fearful either. Use your best judgement and check what the customs are in the country you mean to visit. Learning a little bit of the local language goes a long way towards earning friendship and respect.

Now onto the serious baby backpacking advice! You will need some extra preparation for a baby or very young child, especially in the early stages. You will almost certainly need to prepare more for him/her than for yourself. The most important thing to consider is the means of transport for your little one. This requires at the very least a buggy, and if you intend to do some 'trekking' and what I call 'ruin walking' (for example, wandering among Roman ruins, which usually entails a bumpy ride) I would suggest investing in a light frame that enables you to carry the baby on your back; it is definitely worth it.

Next on your list comes the usual baby paraphernalia, and most certainly do *not* forget nappies. You might be stuck in the middle of nowhere and not be able to find any for sale or be forced to pay a ridiculous price for them. My advice is to count roughly how many you will need for the time spent on your holiday, and stock up. Wherever you go – and this is something I religiously do even for a simple weekend away – bring cough mixture with you, as you will invariably notice that your child needs it. If you do not bring any, some sort of problem is likely to occur all because you are ill-prepared. Obviously where you intend to travel will have a lot to do with this, as it is fairly easy to buy the necessities in most western countries. Even so, you will not want to spend your precious time looking for some open pharmacy in the event that your child starts coughing.

You should also make sure before departure that you have travel insurance – if not for the adults at the very least for the baby or young child who is always more at risk of having an accident or infection.

There is no point skimping on insurance for your child, even on a short trip.

The next crucial item to bring with you is quite a few tins of baby food. That way, you do not need to worry about 'indigenous' food in the country you are visiting – whether it is fresh or not, or whether your child will accept it. It is important to know the source of those tins and to make sure (and this is even more important in hot countries) that you get rid of the leftovers in the baby tin as the heat could get to it very quickly. It is definitely not worth playing with a young child's health by keeping a few mouthfuls in a tin, even for an hour. These precious tins will ensure that he/she will not catch any stomach bug or food poisoning in a different climate, and I cannot stress their importance enough.

Do not forget the insect repellent: cover your child's body with it at night, especially if you stay in a relatively humid area or near a lake or watering hole. This helps avoid a lot of itching the next day, a bad night, and a fair amount of moaning. Another important source of relief in warm/hot countries is a little thermos that you can fill up as you go; be careful with the water you use though. Carrying safe water with you is very useful particularly in places where there might not be any shop around that sells water and where there is not much shade. The thermos will keep your water cool for quite a few hours and keep thirst at bay.

You can certainly take your child to hot countries but you need to be extra vigilant. Children are stronger than we think; after all small children and babies do grow up outside of temperate climates, but do not hesitate but be well prepared. For instance, always keep a T-shirt on them, possibly a special T-shirt like those used by surfers made of a nice clingy material. Their skin is delicate and it goes without saying that the fairer the child, the more fragile they are in the sun. Do not forget a hat for those hotter climates (this is one of the most important things you and your children will need), make sure to avoid the midday sun, and drink plenty of fluids. Always check that the water is bottled when travelling outside of western countries and do not be tempted by those appetizing drinks you might see sold on every corner; they are probably made using unfiltered water. Have a few water purification tablets which can be dissolved in water so as to purify it when you are not sure of its source. As a precaution, if you are unsure of the contents of a bottle, just throw it away. As you gradually become used to the local food, try everything yourself first, and then little by little you can give some to your child. Soup is always one of my favourites and I have never had any problems with it, even in those countries with dubious hygiene standards.

As water has to be boiled for soup, unless the soup brought to you is lukewarm you will be all right and so will your child.

Once you have established what to bring with you and what you can safely do with your little ones, you are halfway there. It sounds more daunting than it actually is. Many people dread bringing their young children on an odyssey of exploration as they believe that the child will not be as interested in sightseeing as an adult. However, believe me, most younger children do find any visit interesting in their own way, more so than a lot of teenagers. Have them look at a ceiling in an ancient castle, or a bird embroidered on some tapestry and you will have captured his/her interest straight away. Take advantage of when they are little (as I have often been told myself for reasons besides travelling); not only do they cost less, they will also want to accompany you anywhere at that time in their life. Unfortunately, this can be a totally different matter when they are older. You will probably give them itchy feet for the rest of their life, and a need to discover their world when they reach adulthood themselves. That is not a bad thing.

So, you now have your tickets, your passports, your plans are in order, and everything is neatly packed for your yearly adventure, but there is a problem: a delay at the airport, a strike, etc. This is not unusual. In fact, you should expect some delays; that way you will not be surprised when they happen. Yes, you know you will need something to distract your child on these long journeys. A colouring book would not be amiss; take a few colouring pencils, a sharpener, a few pens – even a little exercise book will bring joy for many hours. As they get older, they might want to write a diary about their trip – get them involved, it is their trip too! If they have a blanket or a favourite teddy-bear that accompanies them in bed at home, then these must be taken on holiday as well. These familiar things will provide them with a feeling of security and home wherever they are. If everything else fails and your little one refuses to sleep in that strange hotel with all those funny noises outside, sit them in what they know – the wonderful buggy – and that usually does the trick; your little one will fall asleep in the twinkle of an eye. Also bring a few travel games for rainy days or when you have to wait for a couple of hours in some uninviting station or airport.

Now you may think you have all you need, but if you have not prepared for the possibility of your child being car-sick, the mistake will follow you on all those twisting roads and hair-raising bends in the mountains. A simple and useful tool which has a dual function is a bucket; this is much more useful than a plastic bag. As a general rule, if your baby is asleep, do not wake him up to feed him; this is a mistake I have made more than once. He will wake up of his own accord when hunger calls. Forget about set times during holidays, he will not let himself starve.

Now you are ready for the big trip. All this preparation is part of the fun and it is not complicated; it really is not much more difficult than going on a wet and cold weekend in Yorkshire. There is so much less to carry with you if you go to a sunnier climate, and you will come back refreshed and glad you took your baby with you. While he will not remember those happy times until he reaches a certain age, you certainly will. Your child can retrace your steps when he/she is older, and I have found that to be the case with my own children. You will surprise all around you who think you are 'a little bit mad' to be travelling through Turkey, Morocco, Israel, etc., with one or two small children. They might even be envious and wish they could be like you, but as you will soon learn there is no magic; anyone can do it if they are willing to make the effort. Our trips with our first child (and then with our next two children – born five and a half years apart each) took us to various parts of the world, but not as far as we would have liked at the onset, because finances get more stretched the further you go. Nevertheless we travelled to many places that were much different from England. (England was where we lived most of the time, me having followed my husband to his native country.) The experience was definitely worth it each time.

This book focuses on the countries we travelled to on our backpacking trips with the kids. Other trips without our offspring did occur, mostly through my husband's work – but these were another matter and do not figure here. The countries visited with our children include Turkey; Yugoslavia (or rather the former Yugoslavia); Greece and the Aegean Islands; Israel; Tunisia; Mexico; Spain; Morocco; Turkey once more (although this time to another area); Italy; the Peloponnese in Greece; Taiwan; Puglia in Italy; and Sardinia, interspersed with various trips to France (my country of origin) and many others. None of these countries is particularly risky for young children as long as you take the precautions mentioned earlier. I wish to describe, in some detail, a number of these trips to give a general idea of what to expect – not as a touristy guide but rather as a guide to how to behave and what to expect from the natives. I will try to provide a quick impression of the countries generally, always from the perspective of travelling with children. Each country has its own merits, but pointing out the advantages and the disadvantages of each should help you in choosing your destination and avoiding mistakes along the way, making your trip as enjoyable as possible.

Turkey

JULY- AUGUST 1983

The first destination with our first child – then ten months old – was Turkey. We chose Turkey out of a desire for adventure in a place where no one really thought of going back in 1983. The military were still in evidence at the airport, although the country had newly converted to a democracy, albeit a very fragile one at that time. We enjoy places which are not too crowded, where heavy mass tourism has not yet inundated the place with ugly buildings constructed without any thought for the environment. Things have changed since that trip; the country has been transformed and not to its advantage as I have heard that many Turks tend to drag you towards their own restaurant or their cousin's carpet shop, but I believe they are still a friendly people and that Turkey is still a country that people enjoy visiting very much.

When we went in those earlier days there was no commercialism whatsoever. The people welcomed you with open arms, especially if you were with a child as the Turks genuinely love children. Most people there speak a smattering of English and do not try to cheat you out of your money or possessions. In our experience they were very helpful and we still have a soft spot for Turkey and its inhabitants due to their kindness and generosity. Even the taxi drivers knew some English and were very knowledgeable; this was quite humbling! Many women jokingly (or not, who knows) said they wanted to exchange their child for ours – then a little boy with blond curls and eyes the colour of the sea on a beautiful day; quite a rarity there.

Back then, you did not need to be worried when you used the local bus transport as the system was extremely efficient, amazingly cheap, and there was no need to rush to get hold of a seat. Your seat was automatically booked when you bought your ticket, so there was no need to panic. Nobody trampled over you and your children! Another advantage of their excellent bus system was that they offered *eau de Cologne* during the journey – quite a wonderful way to cool down for both the adults and the child, and which left us smelling like a rose. The bus driver also kept a mini-fridge containing bottles of water, so you knew you would have a refreshing trip!

A good point to remember while we are on the topic of transport is that if you are running out of time as we sometimes were in Turkey (being such a huge country), despite being there for a whole month, do not hesitate to use planes – they are an incredibly cheap form of transport there.

Also, make use of the collective taxis which depart as soon as they are full – which hardly takes any time at all! They can get you practically anywhere. You will want to sit in the back of the car though, as they do not seem to have regulations with regards to seat belts; it is much safer for your child this way. You can also hire boats to take you to the myriad islands and unspoilt beaches along the coast of Turkey. With a bit of luck, your 'captain' will stay on board the boat while your child is happily having a siesta, allowing you and your spouse to have a whale of a time in the sea or on the beach.

Turkey and its western coast boast one of the best selections of Roman ruins I have ever seen, and miraculously many of them are situated on the coast. This is a blessing as it means you can do your sightseeing in the morning before it gets too hot and have a swim in the afternoon. This way, you do not get overloaded with visits or beaches – a wonderful combination for the family.

We travelled down from Istanbul (a must). Although the city is an exhausting and crowded place, it is also very exciting and beautiful, with elegant minarets stretching high up to the heavens from its majestic mosques. I would suggest a stay in a fairly luxurious hotel in Istanbul as you could easily end up in a very grotty place otherwise, which is not a very wise thing to do with a young child. In the bedroom, we always made sure that there were soft pillows and blankets placed below the bed in case of a fall.

One touristy tour not to be missed is to take an unforgettable, wonderful boat trip on the Bosphorus, the river separating Europe from Asia. We also took a stroll in the covered souk which is not to be missed either, with its displays of shining wares and maze of covered roads.

There are bargains galore to be had, and don't hesitate to bargain when it comes to price; it is expected. Istanbul itself is a very fascinating city and you need to spend at least four days to get a real feeling of the place. The Blue Mosque is very grand and its gardens are so fresh and beautiful – something our son much appreciated – while the Topkapi Palace is a veritable jewel. Istanbul is another city that never sleeps.

We proceeded to travel down the magnificent Aegean coast, past some truly remarkable archaeological sites such as the well-preserved Ephesus; Pergamon, dangerously perched on a mountain side; the legendary Troy with its huge wooden horse, etc. We went past the Dardanelles which evoke its tragic past; Bodrum with its castle; Kusadashi leading to an inviting sea; Phaselis with its ruins mostly under a growth of pine trees and also under the sea for would-be Jacques Cousteaus; and the wonderful Olu Deniz lagoon, with its warm sea to name but a few glorious places.

Taking the boat across the Aegean Sea can be troublesome however, as we experienced while leaving from the small village of Behramkale to go to a beach on the other side. Keep in mind that the Aegean Sea can be very temperamental, especially during the hottest months of July and August; the Greek legends come to mind. When we reached the Mediterranean coast, the heat started feeling more intense and we relaxed below a castle in Izmir under some shade, sipping hot tea from a silver samovar while our little boy played happily in his buggy, probably quite happy to avoid the heat.

Whenever we left a hotel in the morning he was such a joy to behold, laughing and smiling in our arms at life, ready for another day of adventure. In the evening, we usually went out for a stroll along the coast or had a drink somewhere, our little one fast asleep in his precious buggy, very contented; all the other children were out as well, so there was no need to feel guilty and there was absolutely no point staying indoors. I learnt from that first holiday with our child (and the next ones as well) that a change of routine for a few weeks does not affect your child. Routine is quickly re-established once back home. His life on holiday revolved around us and not the other way round. Naturally this applies as long as you take him into consideration and take a lot of care of his wellbeing; for example, you will not want to be going to a nightclub or anywhere like that.

Ephesus, where St. Paul spoke, is a very eerie place; it is a whole town full of well-preserved buildings, many still standing proudly with its vast theatre, little lizards strolling among the old stones. The heat was very intense and by this stage, our boy's little legs were very brown indeed. We were glad to escape the heat and get closer to the sea yet again soon afterwards. A funny incident happened in the *dollmus* – the collective taxi that we took out of Ephesus – when an old and very dignified man holding the door of our taxi in which he was sitting on a stool suddenly fell out of the moving taxi, finding himself sitting right in the middle of the road with the stool next to him, quite shocked but just grazed and unharmed.

We travelled further south to Marmaris, a picturesque fjord-like harbour with a sea of mountains in the background; the town was swamped by tourists and had numerous cafes and restaurants. At night we made sure we always had water with us if our child woke up thirsty, which happened a few times.

Many times we found the locals to be particularly kind. We arrived in a little town called Fethiye where we visited some beautiful Lycian rocks embedded in the sheer cliffs; there were superb mountains fringing the glorious scenery, and cacti twice my size.

The owner of the place where we were staying took care of our child while we went for a quick swim; there were doors to be seen under the sea of past ruins if you had goggles, which was quite eerie.

We eventually reached one of our last destinations in this incredible trip: Antalya. Here, the heat had become extremely intense and sunbathing was just out of the question – at least in the middle of summer. The best thing to do was to follow our intuition and the natives who knew best. Besides, even sun worshippers like us could not endure such heat, so we stayed in the shade all the time we were on that beach, in the company of whole families picnicking at their tables; it was quite a weird experience! It was so hot that just a short walk to the beach had our buggy melting slightly; I had never experienced such a thing. We experienced something pretty unusual in Antalya's botanical gardens; we saw a yellow rabbit and took a picture as proof we had not dreamt it; this mystery is still not solved to this day.

As time was running out, we took a plane back to Istanbul after a wonderful month spent gazing at so many splendours and living amongst the kindness of the Turkish people and their incessant but well intentioned loving touching of our little boy's head. Even today, Turkey is an excellent destination as it has so much to offer, and you can feel confident about taking your child there. I would recommend it any time and especially for those travelling with children. It is still one of the best places we have visited.

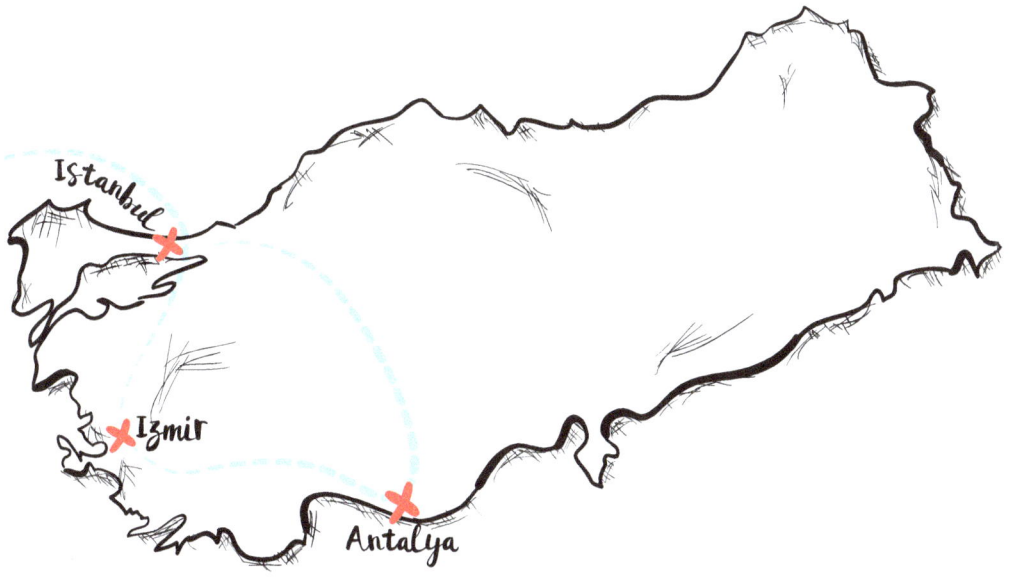

Yugoslavia

JUNE 1984

After some soul searching regarding our next destination for the following year, we decided on Yugoslavia. The same routine was followed for the preparation. As our child grew older though, some things became easier while new problems arose; however, they were definitely not insurmountable problems. You learn by experience and by making mistakes, and as long as you do not play with hygiene and safety with regards to your child's health things usually turn out fine. That always has to be the number one priority.

Yugoslavia proved to be a quite different and beautiful place, with a wonderful rugged coast but hardly any sandy beaches. In fact, most beaches were tiny and often man-made, and therefore quite uncomfortable; you will want to keep this in mind if you are a 'beach bum'. It would be a good idea to bring along some small matted or inflatable mats which will help both parents and children enjoy the beaches more. I must admit we were not prepared for these beaches, but the experience certainly taught me to be so in the future.

Public transport was another matter. We had been spoilt on our last trip; here there was no eau-de-Cologne, and no numerous bus companies to ferry you wherever you wanted. The choice was very limited and the timing of departure awkward. Buses seemed to run at dawn or at sunset and were few in number. This was a hangover from a communist country where everything worked as well as it could. It meant having to be up at the crack of dawn whenever we intended to travel, a negative point when you are tired and you have a sleepy child accompanying you. Still, the effort was worth it. Yugoslavia is an inviting country, and its scenery is lovely. There are some stunning places such as the wondrous Plitvice waterfalls, a unique, one of a kind spectacle consisting of not one but many transparent, limpid waterfalls surrounded by luxurious vegetation.

We arrived first in the north part of the country where we visited the fairly well preserved huge amphitheatre in Pula, a great introduction to the place. We then proceeded to follow the coast south via Opatija, a pretty uninteresting place whose main redeeming factor was a gorgeous beach when it was empty, but being so crowded not a place to get away from it all. Then it was on to the incredible cascade of waterfalls magically falling one into the other.

Do be careful of bites in such a humid atmosphere. We encountered a person who had a family member stung so badly that it necessitated his travelling back to his country in a very poor state of health. Therefore, in any damp area, cover your children in insect repellent and watch them carefully as such areas are bound to be slippery and your little cherubs no doubt will want to run around and be at risk of slipping and falling – which is something our little one did. One advantage of travelling with a baby is that there is no such danger. After that stage in their life, you will need to be constantly vigilant when your child is awake as tourist-type places are often enticing traps where your intrepid child will seek adventure.

Coming back to transport companies, do not listen to their staff, as they were not helpful in the least (although this might have changed). Whenever you see a name on the bus showing the destination you are after, just climb on the bus and do not ask the driver, as he is bound to say that the bus is not going there and then you could be literally stuck somewhere for the whole day.

We then went on to visit Mostar's famous bridge in the Turkish quarter, a magical, enchanting, and delicate piece of architecture that was sadly blown away during the civil war which raged there in the nineties. We have an interesting anecdote linked to this lovely bridge; we bought our little son a pair of typical homemade sandals with some strings attached to the upper sole nearby, which are very unusual. Later on, back home in our small Surrey village – basically the most unexpected place you would imagine this to happen – someone asked me in a shop where I had bought these sandals; she was from Yugoslavia, and even more strange was the fact that we had met her niece on a small island. We have now become firm friends and she has shown us great kindness. Yet whenever we thought of the strange, unfriendly contacts we seemed to have had on a regular basis with the inhabitants, such generous gestures came to mind. I have to say that Yugoslavia did feel tense, but having a child was certainly not a hindrance and probably helped us be treated better than we might have been otherwise. We also met a lovely gentleman – a philosopher – who shared his ideas of the world with us, and I hope he never saw the confusion and horror in his country some ten years later.

The islands in the south such as Hvar and Korcula, with its castle dominating the place, were so pretty. Hvar was almost deserted, with no motorised vehicles authorised. It was very peaceful and laidback in an increasingly fast paced world, and we met an ex-aristocrat there who invited us inside her mansion. You had the feeling of some past glory hidden between those walls and some sense of doom towards the regime – a Communist regime which forbade such luxuries. The place indeed exuded some sadness at not being able to flourish as it should have on such a beautiful, unspoilt island, where time was stood still.

A strange feeling of unease pervaded the whole country with a polarisation of extremely kind gestures on the one hand and some hostility on the other.

We ended the trip in the south, in one of the most beautiful cities in Europe, Dubrovnik, majestically situated on a headland overlooking the Adriatic Sea.

With beautifully preserved walls surrounding the city, Dubrovnik is apparently one of the ten best medieval cities in the world which, looking back, does not surprise me. Every building within the city was so grandiose; these included Gothic, Renaissance, and Baroque churches and palaces, and the famous Onofrio Fountain. Its nickname the 'Pearl of the Adriatic' is certainly deserved, but it has been twice damaged; first during an earthquake in 1667, and more recently during the civil war.

Accommodation in Yugoslavia was rather good for a decent price, and mostly in the shape of bed and breakfasts. Leave the light on for your little child before they fall asleep, as from a certain age they seem to feel the unknown with more intensity. This light and being able to see you around him/her will make them more confident and fall asleep more quickly. We learnt that there was no point struggling and switching the light off with an upset child. Parents can have a quiet talk together and sleep some time later. Once you have ensured the safety, hygiene, and comfort of your child – which is paramount – then you can relax and enjoy yourself, and truly appreciate the privilege of seeing such beautiful places with your child. As in Turkey, we took the bus travelling from Pula in the north to Dubrovnik in the south. We were lucky to experience this country before the tragic events of the civil war. At that time, it was totally safe, but you could sense the unease and tension in the atmosphere.

In order to return to Pula where we had to catch the plane back to Britain, we decided to take a boat, but made a big mistake. We understood that the boat would take nine hours to reach Pula but, to our dismay, it actually took nineteen hours. Panic set in our minds and we asked ourselves how we were going to be able to catch our plane. Well, as luck would have it, we were fortunate enough to find a taxi which drove us at high speed in twisted mountain roads for about 50 kilometres right to the airport. The price of the taxi (thank goodness) was ludicrously low, and we arrived half an hour before departure! This was a stroke of luck, and our little child was unperturbed by it all. I am sure standard taxi fares would have been much more expensive by comparison. This could have been a bad mistake, and it is worth being knowledgeable about trip durations before embarking on some unfamiliar form of transport when you need to catch a plane – a good lesson! ♀

The Aegean Islands

JUNE 1984

Our next destination a year later was Greece and the Aegean Islands. As Greece was then – and still is – quite a popular destination, I would advise booking as early as possible to ensure a cheap return ticket; there is no point hassling over ten pounds, a mistake that I made too often, and in the end it cost me dearly! Greece is a safe place to go to with children and is politically stable; at least it was at that time. Yet again, as in Turkey, children are favourites, but beware; accommodation can and does get full. Reach your destination as early as possible and when you travel round, look for a hotel at once.

This is mostly a Greek Orthodox country, but the Catholic Church also has a large presence on the islands due to the Venetian domination in the Middle Ages. Look out, especially around August 15th, which is the Assumption and a time for big celebrations and holidays, meaning that empty hotels and bed and breakfasts become a rarity. In fact, on one of the islands, we were unsuccessful in finding accommodation and had no choice but to sleep on the beach, something which might not be as tolerated nowadays. Our child, who was by then nearly three years old, was not bothered by this situation however, and was fast asleep all night long in his buggy, gently cradled by the soothing noise of the waves nearby in the warmth of his blanket while we adults hardly slept, huddled in our light sleeping bags on a cold, sandy beach. This just goes to prove the resilience of children while travelling.

So keep this precious buggy for as long as possible; it is so useful. In fact, our child certainly took advantage of it in what seemed a calculating manner to us already. For instance, when we were going downhill, he was very keen to walk. As soon as we were going uphill and the going got tough, he strangely took to his buggy once again with one of us pushing it, sweating profusely under the intense heat of the day.

Another time, we had to settle for a ramshackle place but, yet again, our young child was not bothered. Our hosts were friendly enough, he had some food and a bed, and a little child does not look at his surroundings in the same way as adults. The place was clean if poor. Poverty does not have to go hand-in-hand with dirt and lack of hygiene, although unfortunately it often does.

Athens was unmistakably a sight to wonder at, but I would recommend that you not stay in such a busy town for too long with a very young child because everything becomes more irritating; the heat more torrid; the activity around much more hectic; and moods can change. We had arrived in the night straight from England, and the warmth of the south had immediately swathed us in its veil, but at least it was night time and not such a shock to the system. It helped us to accustom ourselves to the heat which hit us as we arose, awakened by the light shining through the curtains the next morning.

The islands were a delight to the senses. Islands always have that precious element, the wind, which makes for a bearable temperature for you and your child. These islands are all diverse, so it is a good idea to select the ones you intend to visit before you leave home. Some islands are greener; some more for the trendy young people and thus more noisy; some for the nudists, as we experienced once, not realizing it beforehand (I shall always remember the sight of that lady with nothing on bar some scarf on her head); some islands are a blend of magnificent colours such as Santorini, a dream for any photographer, a blaze of ochre, vivid white, deep and tender blue hues all fighting to create a perfect harmony and lure your camera, even more so at sunset. Do not miss the crater on the island opposite that you reach by donkey down rickety, twisted steps, and by boat in half an hour.

We first arrived on the small island of Serifos where we experienced the *meltemi*, a very powerful wind. Everything was swept away by those strong winds, making the place very uncomfortable. Luckily the wind calmed down when we reached the other islands of Sifnos and Milos, peaceful places to do nothing much but rest, admiring the view of the whitewashed villages sitting at the feet of dry, barren brown mountains.

Santorini was most probably the highlight, followed closely by Mykonos, shining with its pure white brightness against the vividly blue sky, its famous windmills, and the excellent ruins of Delos right opposite.

Naxos was also very interesting; a large and so very green island with olive groves and cacti and a very rural charm unlike the others, but we could only visit a part of it. Paros and Naoussa were other interesting islands, not so well known but again with those shimmering white buildings and boats floating gaily on the sea. Santorini was the most spectacular island, with its white houses dangerously perched above the perfect blue sea. It was such a delight to see the colours blending in an incredible sunset, a palette of bright and gentle colours which reflected themselves in our clothes and firing torches of sun in the sea.

Now, you have to remember that these are islands and just because they are situated in the south does not mean that the weather remains the same all the time. Indeed, as mentioned previously, beware the *meltemi* which can blow with severity at certain times in August. The Greeks can be friendly but are possibly less welcoming than the Turks; do not talk about Turkey here though, they are vouched enemies. The welcome I found in Greece was pleasant but more reserved, possibly due to the higher number of tourists flocking there every summer and resultant misbehaviours in ways frowned at by reserved Greeks. Always try to gauge the country, do not abuse it, and respect their ways of life; behave in a good manner appropriate to their religion – this applies everywhere, but more so in some countries. In any case, you are more likely to behave more modestly and moderately when travelling with children, and thus be more appreciated by the natives. There were obviously plenty of beaches for our child to enjoy, and the Aegean Islands are definitely a hit with adults and children for a relaxing holiday with some sightseeing.

Israel

SUMMER 1986

Our next trip was to beautiful Israel which boasts many sights and lovely golden beaches where one can easily alternate visits between tourist sites and suntrap beaches.

However, I would probably not recommend this trip now – and for the foreseeable future – due to the very dangerous political situation with the ongoing bloody conflict between Israel and Palestine. This is a very sad story in a very beautiful country which has managed to conquer the arid land via a wonderful system of irrigation. In peacetime, this was an ideal place for children and adults alike. Even at that time, security was tight and of paramount importance, particularly at the airport. We were asked many questions about our destinations in the country, where even then the possibility of terrorism was never too far away. We were very attentive to the news before embarking on our trip, checking on any slight trouble; this was perhaps one of the last truly safe years to travel there. I thought it was worth mentioning this country for its beauty and the genuine emotions it brings out in its religious aspect, and also because my grandfather had and still owns a square meter of land in Jerusalem.

We arrived in Tel Aviv, a very modern city on the coastline with high-rise buildings which did not detract too much from the lovely place (even though I tend not to like high-rise buildings) as they had quite an original style. The water on the beach of Tel Aviv was an unforgettable experience as its temperature was just like a bath at home and a delight to us all. Beware of sunburn though, as the temperature was very pleasant and you could easily forget that the sun will burn you, especially on your first days after cold England. Do take precautions at the beginning of the holiday and cover your child with a T-shirt when he/she is not in the water, and also limit the time spent in the water because of the exposure to the sun. Always remember that even if the sky is overcast, the sun can still pierce through and sunburn can occur.

We saw some wonderful sights, such as the old city of Acre (which can be seen in the photograph above) with its imposing city walls and where you get the strong impression of being back in Biblical times. The Roman aqueduct of Caesarea was also very impressive and situated right on the beach, a good excuse to mix a 'plunge' in the sea with a great visit.

We bathed in most of Israel's seas bar the Red Sea which was too far south for us to have time to reach on our three week holiday. The Sea of Galilee was lovely and warm at Migdal. We sat on chairs in the sea with the little fishes gently biting at our feet; you could easily imagine Jesus there and the multiplication of the fishes. The Dead Sea – which we visited later on during our trip – was just great for people like me who can hardly swim as it contains so much salt that you can just float on your back; you can actually read in the sea spread out on your back, and it is very safe for your child too. Some tourists covered themselves with the healthy mud, and that was in itself quite a sight!

Of course, we visited the Biblical sights of Jerusalem, Bethlehem, Nazareth, and the fortress of Masada, where the heat was intense. We found that our child – age four then – knew how to take advantage of the shade and the various rests. Intuition seems to protect them, and they always find the best way to avoid the extremes of heat. Always ensure that your thermos of water is filled every morning before you leave your hotel as you might regret it later on if you forget this, although you can and will fill it again at the various water dispensing points. Israel is a safe place regarding food and water, so there is no need to worry.

The intense heat of Masada reminded us that it is definitely worth doing those trips and those climbs uphill when you are still relatively young, so don't wait until your children grow older; you will too! We noticed those older people on package tours and they were really suffering in the heat. Time is never on man's side; the future is unknown and in my experience it is best if you don't put off to tomorrow the trips you can do today – a mistake I will go into in more depth later in this chapter. There are so many gorgeous places to see in the world that you will never be stuck finding destinations to visit, although money limitations might lower your ambitions and you might have to set your sights a little bit nearer to home.

Jerusalem made quite an impression on us with the huge Wailing Wall and the ultraorthodox people leaning and lamenting against the wall; placing little bits of paper in its cracks. One piece of advice: avoid staying in the Mea Shearim, the ultraorthodox area; this was an experience in itself, and you must be very careful with these people as they can become easily offended. Watch what you wear; shorts and short skirts are frowned upon. The ultraorthodox children looked rather weird with their little long locks falling under their black caps and their nearly always bespectacled faces; this is due to too much inter-marrying. You could feel the tension even then between the Israeli and Arab populations.

We were invited for a cup of tea in an Arab house, a very clean and tidy place contrary to what some people say about them. Bethlehem felt calm and quite eerie but much too commercialised, with the long steep road and its mountainous dry backdrop playing host to many shops selling all sorts of things relating to Jesus' birth. Despite this commercialism, the feeling you have when you reach the church, which is supposedly built upon the place where Jesus was born, is quite moving.

We only had one regret when leaving Israel, which was that we had not taken a trip by taxi to the Golan Heights, situated in a lovely green mountainous area where there had been so much fighting, but which was quiet at that time. Money stopped us and honestly, for a sum of 25 pounds or so, it was not worth haggling and refusing a trip to such a famous landmark. Let's face it, one says that one will come back but realistically, one probably does not – or certainly not for a long time – and one should take the opportunity as it arises. I like to think that we learnt from that experience.

We left Israel, full of souvenirs and memories of a wonderful sunny and contrasting country, but one where you could also feel a raw political edge. Our little son loved it. Yet I read again today as I am writing this on holidays about camping with children as being the only viable alternative for families for years to come until these children grow older. This is an example of a thought I just cannot comprehend; children, in my experience, do not want just the beach and pool day in and day out. We, as adults, do not give them enough credit (the same applies in education) and I am convinced that children do appreciate novelty and sightseeing intermingled with beaches. To my mind anyway, clever children want to discover places and will get bored just as much as adults with beaches and sunbathing alone. As far as having children kept motivated by playing organised games on the beach with some instructors, yes, it is fine for a while, and there are times when a couple likes to be on their own. But I also believe that a holiday is a time for the family to rediscover themselves and take time together, as a rushed daily routine might not allow that to happen during the year. Holidays are a good time to get closer and when you are a family unit alone in a foreign country, not surrounded by your neighbours from home, the protective instinct in the parents brings the family closer together. This is also true when you happen to live abroad. A more adventurous holiday tends to bring you very close and you wish you could stop time and save these precious moments alone with your children, and that bring you close to the people of the country you are visiting.

Tunisia

SUMMER 1987

Tunisia was our next holiday destination; this was our first encounter with North Africa, and we knew we had to be careful as far as water was concerned. Armed with my usual guide and with double precautions, we headed towards the airport, laden with the same faithful little rucksacks and the *passe-partout* bag, which contained sandwiches and biscuits – a safety measure before setting foot on that mysterious continent.

Tunis welcomed us with the usual smells of hot countries, enveloping us in slight trepidation and apprehension. Tunis itself was quite a grand place – which we did not expect – with large avenues dotted with tall palm trees gently swaying under the hot sun. One of our first visits, however, was to a rather sad-looking zoo where the animals seemed half dead, which was a great shame as this could have been a good introduction to the fauna inhabiting the shores of North Africa. Besides, zoos are always a favourite with kids. The town itself was interesting and we were shown around by a Tunisian dressed in his long traditional robe. The first stop was above the town, and there were some lovely blue tiles covering the capital's mosques, shining in a myriad of colours in the bright sunlight. I read in our guide that if Tunisian men wore flowers on one side of their head – I forget which side – that meant they were gay, and these gay men held hands unashamedly. Quite a surprising sight in what is after all an Islamic country where, for instance, even kissing in public is frowned upon.

Tunisia is a multifaceted country in its range of sightseeing, from the lovely, quaint blue and white Sidi Bou Said – a very touristy place but so beautiful against the blue sky and well worth the detour – to the Roman ruins of famous Carthage.

Bulla Regia, with its magnificent underground villas with their well-preserved mosaics; the jewel that is the amphitheatre of El Djem; brilliant white romantic Hammamet shimmering in the sunshine; Nabeul, famous for its pottery and camel market; the impressive buildings at Sousse, with its old ribat contrasting with the nearby modern complex of Port El Kantaoui; the grand mausoleum at Monastir dedicated to Bourguiba, the ex-president whose name adorns most cities of Tunisia; the grand mosque of Kairouan … there is so much to see that the list goes on and on. The south was also quite different, with its many oases where pomegranates, fig trees, and olive trees abound.

Also of interest are the Matmata underground dwellings where some of *Star Wars* was filmed. Then you have the long blonde beaches of Djerba Island. Tunisia is a place with something to suit every taste and every age, pleasing child and adult alike. One piece of advice is to be extremely careful when walking up the steps of the ribat (castle), as they are often uneven and one could end up with a badly sprained foot – as was the case for my husband, to the great joy of our son, when he fell. However, this could mar any holiday and could happen to anyone; luckily, this was towards the end of all our walking.

Another important consideration when travelling in Tunisia – and this, of course, is even more valid with small children – is that you need to be extremely careful with food and drink; never drink tap water, beware of uncooked vegetables, and choose your restaurants with extreme care. Try to avoid those where small skeleton-like cats hang around; they might not have very safe hygiene. If you have been going to some restaurant and have had no tummy problems there, it might be a good idea to return to that place and not be too adventurous. Again, my husband got sick when we went to a restaurant which our guide specifically said to avoid, so also follow the advice given by your guide. As long as you are vigilant, you and your family should be all right.

Transport was no problem as far as I can recall; trains were efficient thanks to the French who installed them, and there was the possibility of renting jeeps to go in the desert, something which would have been exciting but for which we did not have enough time, seeing as we had intended to spend a week on Djerba Island to have a rest from all our trekking around the country.

We proceeded to take a break from backpacking as we were to go and live in the United States for a couple of years. This was lucky in a way as our second child was born in the spring and backpacking with a four month old baby is not really advisable. The experience of living abroad was most interesting and both parents and children had to adapt to a hot climate after the cold, windy, and damp English days. This proved quite a challenge and even though there was no backpacking, it showed us the incredible adaptability of young children to different places and climates. In fact, the younger the better, as they do not miss friends so much then, and appreciate the whole experience much more. It shows once again that you can take children abroad, especially young ones, for any length of time and never need to fear the unknown, but rather cherish this as a great chance to live something different and develop one's sense of adventure in the process.

In the end, anybody should broaden their mind along with their horizons whenever possible.

Mexico

AUGUST 1989

As our next holiday was looming on the horizon once more, an opportunity not to be missed was to visit some Central or South American country. We had looked round for some relatively cheap prices but most of the flights to the West Indies were very pricy, and we turned towards our second option: South or Central America. Again, South America turned out to be disappointingly expensive. So our best bet and most obvious destination since we were living in Texas was to be Mexico. Thus far, we had only been to a couple of border towns for the day, but even they already looked so different from Texas, with large empty avenues leaving room for smaller roads busy with people walking, and plazas in the middle. Why we did not think of Mexico in the first place beats me. This was a place which had always fascinated and tempted us, but we were hoping to reach more distant destinations from where we were. As it turned out, Mexico was the ideal place to visit. I dread to think of the cost of visiting such an idyllic, fascinating place with two children when starting from Great Britain. We would not have been able to afford it and to miss such an opportunity would have been pure madness. As it was, the flights from Texas were relatively inexpensive and we were to see quite a lot of this huge country in a fairly short time – two and a half weeks that we had been able to put aside from my husband's holiday entitlement. Indeed, holiday entitlement in the United States is not the best, though there are many other advantages to life there, such as the low cost of living.

Mexico, here we are! We had to be doubly vigilant regarding food and drink, and we had a young child with us once again along with our six-year-old son, who was by then less vulnerable. Thus, we stuck to our usual trick of bringing plenty of baby food tins and nappies. We bluntly refused to drink non-bottled water, and were not even tempted to touch any salad. This time, there were four of us on this great adventure flying to Mexico City, one of the most populous capitals in the world. Mexico City greeted us with rain, but the temperature was still nice and quite warm – although cool after Texas. We arrived in time to see some sort of ceremony with people flying along totems, listening to the rhythmic tam-tam of some mysterious chiefs in their Indian attire.

In Mexico, we saw many contrasts: the poor *favellas* or slums outside Mexico City, and the very richly decorated city of Oaxaca, shining in its own golden splendour. A few kilometres away from Mexico City was the old city of Teotihuacan which we reached by taxi; this was a very good deal and what is more, the taxi waited for us without charging further expenses. We climbed the steep steps of the Pyramid of the Sun and of the Moon among people unscrupulously showing off their ancient wares to tourists.

We left Mexico City to visit the Yucatan Peninsula and its marvels by plane. One must not forget that Mexico is a huge country and the distances involved are enormous. Bus transport would be lengthy and possibly dangerous with regards to thieves, as we were informed later on. In Mexico, do not hesitate to use planes as they are – or at least were back then – incredibly cheap. It was literally the first time that we could take planes as we would usually take buses; all planes fly via Mexico City where we had to change or wait before the plane took off for any other destination.

Yucatan is such a mosaic made up of numerous Aztec pyramids and beautiful sights, and we had to decide which ones to visit in our limited time there. Uxmal was on our list of must-sees, along with Chichen Itza. Those sites we visited on an organised trip for once, as time was not in our favour and the price for the visit to these two sites – and being ferried here and there by minibus – was so low. This was something I had not seen before as in most European countries, and even some like Turkey, most organised trips were costly, and this went for the poorer Mediterranean ones too. This probably reflected the poverty of many people in Mexico, and what we spent for this organized trip would represent a huge amount of money for many of its citizens. However, to take advantage of a day of relaxed sightseeing at such a low price was too tempting, and hopefully would help people in the country. Tourism, if well managed, is often a great help to enriching a country's economy and thereby its people, as long as you do not flash your 'riches' disrespectfully.

We were able to experience a beautiful sight at Xel Ha, an area of blue transparent lagoons where 'zebra' fish could be watched with the help of a scuba mask. Tulum was another wonderful place to visit, a maze of Mayan ruins along white sands and inviting sea. I forgot to mention that we were able to contemplate gorgeous views from the plane going to the Yucatan, flying over the jungle; quite a dream made reality for many an adventurer. The children loved all those pyramids dedicated to some long forgotten gods, where atrocities had been committed to fulfil some god's bloodthirsty desire. Stories were still abounding of young women being left to survive in the jungle and possibly being devoured by jaguars.

There were countless other sights to be seen but unfortunately for us, time had run out and we had to be selective. Otherwise, Palenque would have certainly been worth a visit, but it was less accessible and required a much longer bus trip to reach it. Anyone with plenty of time should probably go to Guatemala in peaceful times, as there are other archaeological sites there which lie deep in the jungle but require a couple of days' bus drive to reach – a long distance with little kids, but not an impossible task.

So we left mystical Yucatan for 'mainland' Mexico with our usual transport, the winged one which took us over the Popocatepetl Mountains covered with snow, and headed for Playa del Carmen for a well-deserved rest. This little place is situated along an idyllic pale blonde beach with matching pale blue sea and palm trees throwing their welcoming shade on a Caribbean-lookalike paradise; an ideal beach for children. We had not been able to reach the Caribbean yet but we had found something similar in a yet undiscovered part of Mexico.

Unfortunately, some building construction was already on its way in this tiny resort, which was so appealingly unknown; most American tourists headed for ugly and expensive Cancun. At the time I am writing this, this slice of paradise which was Playa del Carmen has been discovered by tourists, unfortunately.

We did not want to depart from our bit of paradise which we left with mixed feelings to travel onto Oaxaca, the city of gold. Oaxaca is an old city, bejewelled with cathedrals covered with gold in a country where poverty is rife; there were people weaving in the streets to sell their wares, and shanty towns and huts appearing here and there in the countryside, providing quite a contrast! There were more ruins to be seen on the outskirts of Oaxaca on Monte Alban, in fresh mountain scenery.

Then it was on to Acapulco with its tourist traps and plenty of pestering timeshare-selling 'sharks'. A piece of advice; avoid them like the plague, as we experienced (to our regret) a lot of time being wasted on some silly idea that we were not going to follow up anyway. High-rise towers dominate the wonderful bay of Acapulco. An impressive spectacle was to see the brave young divers do their plunge from those fantastic cliffs in the sunset, quite an awesome, unforgettable sight at the end of our Mexican adventure. However, Acapulco could have turned into a nightmare for the adults if not the children. We were so careful with the children that perhaps, as time went on, we tended to forget our vigilance for ourselves.

My husband decided on some appetising fish in a restaurant which looked fine; one could be forgiven for thinking that this place was unlike other Mexican towns as it looked more like a European resort, and thus drop their guard. He was to regret having ever eaten that fish as he started feeling unwell soon after, and this lasted for a few weeks after the trip, with some associated muscular problems. The hotel also served us some water which was uncorked, which we had not been aware of, and we felt slightly uncomfortable after having drunk it. To cap it all, I nearly drowned in a swimming pool on the shores of the Pacific, which was not so pacific indeed. So much for Acapulco!

Also, another piece of advice not mentioned so far; do be even more careful towards the end of any trip, as that is the time when problems can occur as we relax our ways, and be doubly vigilant with your children. You do not want Montezuma's revenge – or any revenge for that matter – and this obviously is even more important for the ones under your protection.

New York, Boston and Niagara Falls

SEPTEMBER 1990

The summer after that was an interlude as regards backpacking as we stayed around some of my husband's family near New York and Boston on the way back from the States to the UK. So, for once we let ourselves be guided and also had a day by ourselves making our way through the forest of buildings that is New York City, going up to the top of the famously doomed Twin Towers, for instance. I would just like to briefly mention this holiday, although it was not strictly backpacking.

The Italian side of the family welcomed us with open arms and showed us around the most famous parts of where they lived in Boston. We visited one of the oldest sites to be seen in the U.S., Plymouth Plantation, where the Quakers first arrived in the 1600s. The whole site was beautifully reconstructed and the pretend inhabitants were dressed as in the old days and seemingly lived as people had in the old days; we were really transported into those years, and it was quite magical. Then, of course, we visited Boston whose oldest parts are very charming.

We also visited the famous Martha's Vineyard Island, where the rich and famous still go. Then, of course, there was a necessary visit to New York; we went round the Statue of Liberty on the free ferry; past Trump Tower and Hyde Park, and to finish the trip we travelled to the wonderful Niagara Falls, where we had to wear some yellow raincoats as the weather was terrible. But it somehow made for a better atmosphere with the mist floating around those most impressive falls. Afterwards, it was back to good old Britain, which met us a few months later with some horrible blizzards; nothing better to cause one to dream once again of hotter climates where T-shirts and shorts are de rigueur.

WE WERE BACK THAT SUMMER TO BACKPACKING IN

Andalucia, Southern Spain

SUMMER 1991

I was lucky enough to have a distant cousin living near Malaga where we landed, which meant the first two nights were stress free. Otherwise, we had as a rule started to book our first night's (or two) accommodation before leaving Britain, as we were now four people needing a room. This meant we did not have to be at the mercy of any 'crook' who wanted to take us to his 'grotty' hotel at the time of our arrival. This being in search of beds might be awkward at the best of times since we usually arrived at our destination quite late, as these were the cheapest flights available. We could therefore begin our trip rested, with our minds free of worries.

One or two days in a foreign country will make it easier to find accommodation on the spot, because by then you have become more accustomed to the way of life and know what to expect. Indeed, you quickly get to know what price you need to pay for a decent hotel or bed and breakfast depending on the country you are visiting – something which even guidebooks cannot really give you an idea of. It offered us peace of mind; also, generally speaking the hotels you can phone (and now book on the Internet) are usually of a fairly good standard if they, for instance, offer a fax number. Having said that that, you could also be totally mistaken even with Trip Advisor, which is the norm now; still, by booking ahead you assure yourselves of a couple of beds and that has to be better than nights under the stars.

Your adventure still starts when you leave your home and the big thrill is certainly when you set foot on that land with wafts of fragrant air welcoming your nostrils. Now, the Costa del Sol has long been known for its nightlife spots such as Torremolinos, but there is another Andalucia which just waits to be explored with its three main centres of interest. These are Seville, Granada, and Cordoba – but there are also many other, lesser known places which sometimes should be left a secret.

Nightlife seemed to have taken a toll anyway as Spain had become a more expensive country to visit; a good thing in some respects but also a bad thing for our purse, which had to be stretched that much further.

The hotels were indeed rather pricey, and we had to make do with smallish hotels which were still rather expensive and often situated in noisy areas. You must not forget that the Spanish people like to get out at night, and are a rather nocturnal people. Since they had a siesta in the afternoon, come the evening they are ready to have fun and enjoy outdoor life with their noisy bikes until three o' clock in the morning! So if possible choose a hotel on a cul-de-sac if you want to have a decent sleep; the noise could be a real nuisance!

Some of our first sights were of Puerto Banus, the St Tropez of Andalucia, with its rich marble apartments glimmering over the cacti, and palm trees fringing their front right on the beach. We know where the tax dodgers live! The port was a maze of yachts competing with each other in their grandeur. As you went inland, the most impressive cliffs of Ronda imposed themselves on you with their natural beauty intermingling with the local architecture, dangerously perched around their chasm. The town felt peaceful and although quite well known, it did not seem to attract many tourists; we more or less had the place to ourselves, which we did not complain about. Soon after that day, we went to see some ancient paintings in some *cuevas*, again inland. The transport to reach the place was not fantastic; we managed to get there, but there was nothing to get us back to the coast. Luckily, a British couple noticed us and gave us a lift back, which helped us tremendously as I am not sure that taxis even came there unless you called them in advance. The place was almost deserted, a strange occurrence for such a spot where you could have a glimpse of authentic prehistoric paintings, something impossible now in Lascaux in Southwest France. This showed us that if you ever become stuck in the middle of nowhere with or without kids, there is always a way to return to your base. We have had to hitchhike with the kids in tow on quite a few occasions.

We then travelled on to Tarifa, where the Mediterranean and Atlantic meet; a pretty but costly town, hence its name or so it seemed to us. Gibraltar was then to entice us back to a British enclave in the sun, a little town struggling to find some room below that huge rock for its inhabitants. All the shops there were those that you would find anywhere back in the UK, and the place was full of life and trepidation; a little England in the sun, and a worthwhile visit contrasting with the rest of the Costa del Sol. I envied its inhabitants for having both England and Spain on its doorstep, and their bilingual abilities.

After that, we went on to a jewel of a place which we were happy to discover and which then was not on the tourist route, although now it has been mentioned in a few travel brochures, which is a great shame! This gem called Cadiz (actually famous in a French song) breathed a gentle air with endless miles of empty white sands only frequented by Spanish people. The city itself abounded with majestic buildings and narrow streets leading to a large square and an odd cathedral with rude statues. We could not leave beautiful Cadiz without wandering in its garden and, of course, having a peck under the Tree of Love.

Our next port of call was beautiful, hot Seville. The heat was indeed very intense and reminiscent of Texas, but the sweaty tour of it – albeit walking from shade to shade – was worth the detour. The sculptures of its cathedral, and the *giralda* with its Ottoman architecture, were exquisite; the intricate work done to build these marvels must have required a monumental tour de force and patience. We had to go and see Christophe Colombo's tomb inside the cathedral; of course, whether it actually is his last resting place in reality remains to be seen as many places on earth claim to be his birthplace or the place where he is resting. The Alcazar was a *chef d'oeuvre* with wonderful Ottoman architecture once again, showing the prowess of these people, their characteristic details engraved on the stones. Then it was onto another imperial city, Cordoba, whose main attraction is its incredible cathedral with numerous columns inside called the *mezquita*, a forest of columns mixing Christian and Muslim architecture. This wonder was nearly destroyed and as there is nothing like it in the world, that would have been a great shame! Not far from the cathedral on the other side of a Roman bridge, the Tower of La Calahorra was rising, a tower dedicated to the Muslim faith. It would be nice if both religions were at peace with each other!

We went back to the coast for some rest from our inland sightseeing with very patient children in one of the hottest places in Europe, before going on to incredible Grenada, nestling below snow-capped mountains, and possibly the highlight of the holiday, the majestic Alhambra.

An important point to make here to show the advantages of independent travelling over package tours is that a place like the Alhambra deserves the time it takes to see it in all its splendour. The package tours we saw going there visited this gorgeous place in two hours and then off they went back on the bus for another quick tour of Seville maybe, or to go to some restaurant.

As for us, we visited in freedom at our own pace and actually spent two days exploring this amazing site. The views from almost anywhere left you gazing in wonder, from turrets down the valley to the peaceful gardens with their delicate columns; the ponds glistening and bringing freshness in the inner courtyards and fountains; the fragrant flowers throwing red, yellow, and orange flashes of colours onto the scenery among the bushes; growing into the rockery. Two hours would definitely not do justice to the Alhambra; you have to savour the atmosphere.

We reluctantly left Grenada to go back to the coast via the lovely whitewashed village of Salobrena, crowned with an Ottoman fortress defending the town, and stopped in Nerja, the so-called balcony of Europa, a lovely spot with some truly wonderful views. However, the smells at certain times were rather off-putting due to the high number of tourists, which slightly marred the whole place and made one a bit hesitant to swim in the otherwise inviting water.

After this lengthy description of Spain in which I somehow lost myself such was its beauty, I wanted to show that a trip based mostly on a lot of sightseeing, such as this one, was still achievable without any problems with children in tow; there were no complaints to be had. 📍

Morocco

SUMMER 1992

We headed off to Morocco on our next holiday, having once before tasted the sweet delights of Northern Africa, and which were beckoning again. Morocco is a large country with many sights, and we had to make a choice once again about what we were going to visit. We therefore decided on a visit to the imperial cities, leaving the Atlas Mountains and the desert for another visit. As I mentioned earlier, with time limiting access to some places, it is worth considering in advance what can be realistically visited without rushing around. This is even more important with children.

Morocco opened itself to us firstly at the well-known and well visited Agadir on the Atlantic coast. Because of the sea air, the temperature was extremely pleasant, hovering around 26 degrees; this was a gentle introduction to Morocco, and the white palm tree-lined beach flanked by the ever present mountains was immense and stretched on for miles. The vegetation was plentiful with pink and white oleanders and bougainvilleas gently covering unexpectedly green grassy areas. After a couple of days relaxing in Agadir, we were on the road once more, taking the bus to the inland magical, Biblical town of Taroudant.

Public transport here was not so efficient but amusing at times, so you need to arm yourself with patience and take plenty of water with you. This supposedly short trip took forever in an old rickety bus with the driver stopping en route ... to have a sandwich, after which he proceeded to play football! Still, Taroudant was worth the trip as it remained untouched by modern civilisation; you enter the walled town and make your way through a maze of narrow streets full of traders, artisans beating hot irons, dye stalls, and jewellery-makers with spice aromas filling the air. The young man beating the hot iron had muscles as hard as a rock, a trait that you do not encounter much nowadays outside the boxing ring, although the gym has become a place where young men aspire to develop huge but not so attractive muscles, whereas this person had earned these muscles through hard work. In the middle of this incredible out-of-this-world place, we managed to find a lovely, very comfortable hotel with a swimming pool thrown in at a very decent price. We even went in a *caleche*, a horse-drawn carriage for the few tourists like us, to the delight of the kids. We could not usually afford such a promenade as prices in many places around the world for such a luxury are usually insanely high.

We then headed for Marrakech and stopped en route at a little village with a lovely hotel stuck in the middle of nowhere where, in fact, my parents had been a few years before; it was quite emotional for me to be there in the same place. The landlady was French, and married to a Moroccan man. We had a great meal with the other 'customers' in the open-air in the yard, and that was really convivial. The next day, we had a look at some pottery on the other side of the road; the pottery and precious gems were rather pleasing to the eye, and so cheap. Goaded on by curiosity, we also visited the hinterland and walked on some paths in wooded areas by the back of the hotel.

Suddenly, little children appeared from nowhere and were surrounding us. They looked rather poor, walking barefoot among the trees and were begging us in French for some money and some biscuits. Some of them managed to have us follow them, telling us to come and visit their home. Their home was a humble home indeed, nestled into some high rocks; pitch black, a kitchen open to the skies where there were a few kitchen utensils, a small room where a small table was laden with glasses for us by the mother who made us some tea. Flies were raging around us, but they did not seem to notice. The young mother showed us the bedroom, a dark room with a simple bulb which was not working, plain rough walls with no wallpaper or paint on them, and some sleeping bags on some mattresses on the hard floor – this was their home. In the luxury of our hotel just about next door, we were feeling somewhat guilty. I had never seen such a place, yet we had previously entered some poor houses where hygiene was dubious, but such barrenness of a house with no door, no enclosed kitchen, and yet smiling faces in front of adversity gave us something to think about. I believe we gave them some money, but I distinctly remember giving the pack of biscuits that I was holding as they certainly needed them more than us. Another thing to remember when visiting these countries is to have biscuits or pens with you; children around the world always appreciate such little gestures. Having children ourselves with us might have helped us get out of situations which could have been awkward. Back at the hotel, our next surprise was a tamed stork living among the customers. What a lovely bird; it had apparently been injured and then rescued.

We left this unforgettable place by shared taxi the next day to reach magical, mythical Marrakech. Although Marrakech was not very distant, the road to it was very twisty and it took about three hours; some of us did not feel too good by the end of the ride. The most spectacular place in Marrakech has to be the Jemaa El Fna square, a huge square whose name means 'the place of the dead', where people were executed in the past.

The place is definitely mystical, and somewhat frighteningly eerie as dusk came, and it filled with all sorts of people: old women beggars draped in black whose small stature only showed twisted, wrinkled, witch-like hands asking for money; monkeys on other beggars' shoulders, which they tried to place on you; snake charmers ... and the square became full of more and more weird people of all ilk – time to go! Before the evening, the same square oozed charm and it was a pleasure to have a drink and watch the passers-by, but as the evening wore on, it was a different matter altogether and probably not a good idea to stay on with little children in your charge. We had an afternoon visiting the medina in Marrakech, following our self-appointed guide who himself became aggressive when he changed his mind at the end of our tour, asking us for more money. Marrakech was a fascinating city, definitely worth the visit, but it is a place to be wary of, where one has to be on one's guard.

Some distance away, the impressive Ouzoud waterfalls were worth the detour, quite a long detour, in some strangely fresh place near Ilfrane, known as the little Switzerland of Morocco, where the kings had their palaces to get away from the relentless heat of the imperial cities. The buildings themselves looked Swiss and we were transplanted in another world and able to have a break from the hot Moroccan summers, which was good and refreshing for the whole family. We rested by a pool in those idyllic surroundings like a royal family ourselves.

Then came the visits to Fes and Meknes, the other two most important imperial cities in the country, and we were back to the implacable heat and the usual guides, probably the plague of Morocco, although our guide in Fes was very friendly and interesting. Those buildings were quite fantastic with their beautiful ochre walls and towers lending themselves to the tapestry of markets and medinas in which people hurried, doing tasks which had been done since the dawn of time. Volubilis charmed us with its beautifully preserved Roman ruins – a change from ribats and mosques. Of course, we could not leave Morocco without visiting its capital, Rabat, with the impressive white structure that constituted the mausoleum of Mohammed V, glimmering under the azure skies. We also spent an afternoon in its memorable tropical gardens, a jungle-like greenery where we felt like Tarzan, crossing rickety wooden bridges, and gazing at tortoises on huge lilies in green waters – a great ending to a fascinating country which had much to offer. The children were fantastic travellers, and seemed to enjoy it greatly and take it all in their stride.

Turkey: Cappadocia and the Black Sea

AUGUST 1993

Turkey dawned on us again, but this time another area – the Black Sea area – which was not so well (and still probably is not) trod by tourists, and the famous Cappadocia area, which is much more visited. I was pregnant with our third child and we had decided to give time to our little girl on her own before the baby's arrival; our boy – only age ten – was sent to his uncle in France. In hindsight, he was really a brave boy to fly on his own without complaining, a characteristic which should help him all through his life. I was halfway through my pregnancy and since everything was going well, we set off to explore the famous Cappadocia Mountains – which we missed the last time as Turkey is such a vast country – and the unspoilt Black Sea area. We had a fair idea of the country by then and knew what to expect more or less; the welcome that we had in the remotest parts yet undiscovered by tourism is still something to cherish, which shows that kindness and generosity are still part of this harsh world. Needless to say, as mentioned on our previous trip to Turkey, children are loved in this country and you could not choose a better place to bring children on holiday. Our little Vivienne was carried in everybody's arms and enjoyed every minute of it, although she might have been overcome at times.

We flew to Ankara, the capital, where we were welcomed by … well, not the sun as you would expect in this part of the world, but by a rainy and chilly night. It slightly dampened our spirits and the start of this holiday; the rain was rather unexpected since they had been having a drought. We had booked a hotel from home back in England and hailed a taxi in Ankara to drive us to the place, only to be told that the room had gone as we had arrived after midnight. This was rather disappointing and left us worried about how to ever find a hotel at this late time. We were lucky enough to find a fairly grotty room in a nice hotel where the man spoke some English and took pity on us. This room was not ready but being redecorated; there was only one double bed where the three of us huddled, grateful for having a roof over our heads.

The fact that we had a child with us probably helped us getting the room. We had two more nights in that hotel and were given two lovely and comfortable rooms after that first night for 25 pounds, so that was all worth it. We had a good chat with the owner whose wife was Welsh, which explained his good English. This was actually the most we were going to pay for rooms during this trip – not bad!

Ankara is after all the capital, a strange place where poverty and slums stand shoulder to shoulder with fashionable streets with well-dressed people going about their business. The archaeological museum was situated on a hill overlooking squalor, and yet was a haven full of rich finds and shining with cleanliness. The centre of the town was adorned with new buildings surrounding a beautiful park with water features everywhere. By then, the heat had reclaimed its territory; it was pretty intense and had started slowing us down. That refreshing water glimmering under heavy Turkish skies was a delight after all!

Our first leg of the journey after having visited the capital was to be the gorgeous eerie-like Cappadocia, with its incredible mountains folding like vertical sand dunes, and with ex-troglodyte habitations. Its whole atmosphere and changing colours were simply breathtaking, out of this world. The white orangey peaks turned to purplish-pink as dust came, shrouding the place with awesome mystery and beauty. We had a whole day to ourselves just wandering among those fantastic shapes; and we had an encounter which could have been rather troublesome ... a huge snake as large as any I had never seen before in the wild.

My husband was busy ahead of us taking pictures while my little girl and I were lagging behind when we heard that unmistakeable *sshh* sound.

However, we did not panic and just looked at the long creature zigzagging around at a metre's distance from us, busily heading to its destination. I somehow realised that this snake was not going in our direction and we just stopped in our steps, not wanting to disturb the fellow. Luckily our daughter took it all in her stride and did not shout or utter any sound, which was probably just as well. So, a good piece of advice is to trust nature and disturb it as little as possible.

We explored the next day in another part of Cappadocia, booked with a tour this time, and found ourselves trotting around those white cliffs with a group of French people, discovering some remnants of churches still adorned inside some caves.

En route, we met a group of Turkish farmers and families with their sheep who took a shine to our daughter; they placed her on a donkey and whispered sweet words to her which she obviously could not understand, but their nature was charming. Some wore typical traditional clothes which looked rather pretty (see photo on a previous page), and this was a better encounter than the previous day's had been. We sadly left this wonderful area where we could have easily spent a week. The hotels were also so cheap and plentiful, as this was tourist territory but the sort of tourism which is not on a grand scale for avid travellers like us.

We headed towards the Black Sea, stopping en route at Siva, a town that I would not necessarily recommend, although still an interesting stopover to break up the journey. This was ultra-Islamic territory and my shorts were not regarded as an item of clothing which I should be wearing in this part of the world. An old lady gave me a long, frowning look which did not impress me; I am glad that she was old as her eyes seemed to be hitting me. This area was known for being anti-liberalism, whereas some other parts of Turkey were more 'Europeanised'. A hotel in Siva which housed some poets from all over the world had burnt down in a deliberate fire not so long ago, killing some of the residents just because they had more liberal views of the world. This left a rather chilling impression, and you could feel a heavy atmosphere of distrust of strangers as I have not experienced anywhere else in this country.

This was just a stopover and we were glad to leave the next day to breathe a more liberal air on the Black Sea, arriving in beautiful, romantic Amasya with its typical wooden houses built below the mountains and facing the river, Lycian tombs overlooking them. There we were to encounter a lot of kindness (very humbling indeed) as we were further along the Black Sea coast and in virtually non-tourist country despite its beauty. My touristic guide featured a lovely hotel with an inner yard and flowers sprouting from everywhere. Our cheap room did not reflect the beautiful design of it; our bed sheets were hand woven, matching the long red curtains, and it looked as if we were in a luxury Bedouin tent. The bathroom was tucked away behind some creamy doors, giving the impression that there was no bathroom behind them; this was the wonderful work of the owner who was also an architect and had given vent to his talents. Our little child was as much appreciated here as in the other places and had made friends with the owner's daughter and their Lassie dog. The next day, we went off exploring some ruins of a castle perched above the town, quite a steep ascent and, luckily for me, we had a lift with some policemen who must have had some time off and took some pity on us. I was a little apprehensive with those three men at first but, of course, they were harmless and very kind.

The view from those ruins was truly fantastic, with the river meandering below, glimmering among red roofs alongside the elevated columns of the mosques. We slowly walked back down some huge old steps, and were by the river when we were approached by some people: "Weren't you at the bank this morning? We looked for you all day; you have left your passport there."

I had not remembered having left my passport and with many thanks accepted my passport back with such relief. What a mess we would have been in had we left the place, and if they had not bothered to look for us even when their bank was closed. How many bank employees would have looked for their customers back in Britain, not having a clue where we were staying or what we were doing?

We left this beautiful town with regret to get back towards the coast and a more cosmopolitan place where we met some Americans with whom we had a drink and a chat at the place they were renting.

At our next port of call, we were helped by a young boy about ten years old, who spoke some English and helped us find a hotel; he also took us back to his family's home, where we had lunch. We reached another little town some time later via a small bus zigzagging quickly on hairpin curves on top of the forested cliffs with beautiful vistas on the Black Sea. This was totally unspoilt scenery; the bus was so crowded that two people were travelling on top, their feet dangling over the sides in precarious positions, or so it seemed to me. The sweat was pouring down on our bodies and it was good to have a short respite in this lovely countryside and breathe some fresh air. We finally arrived at our destination, a little port where we found accommodation pretty easily. This was quite a touristy place in comparison with the last one and we decided to go on a boat trip to see some waterfalls on the other side.

We were delighted when the boat went at long last, giving us some welcome breeze. We stopped where the waterfalls were located and crossed some deserted Robinson Crusoe-like island with jungle all around us and fresh cool streams among the dense vegetation.

On our way back, our little boat ran out of petrol; the Robinson Crusoe adventure was carrying on! Thus we were stranded in the middle of the sea and our captain hailed a fishing boat which took us on board. Allan and the captain had to carry me from our little craft to this fishing boat right in the middle of the sea, and I was quite a weight with the little life inside me. Eventually we were all safe and sitting among the fishing nets – quite an adventure! We met a couple of Danish people and had a drink with them later on. They were very friendly and, in fact, we still wrote to each other for a long time every Christmas. Their family size increased as well since they were only two of them then, and I wonder whether they carried on travelling in the same way.

At the end of this beautiful trip we ended up in Safranbolu, a traditional wooden inland town; indeed, these wooden houses were very beautifully carved and this was a nice end to our second Turkish trip. We had a drink in a gorgeous hotel with the owner or representative, and this hotel was adorned with the most exquisite traditional décor. Our Turkish trips have always been a source of wonder not only because of the nature of its buildings but also because of the nature of its people, and I definitely recommend Turkey for any trip with children. They are always welcoming you and, in fact, oftentimes invite you to meet their families.

A PAUSE FROM BACKPACKING IN

Brittany and Normandy

SUMMER 1994

We then had a break from backpacking, but I hasten to say not a break from holidays. This would have been tantamount to a crime to me; a year without going on holiday is equivalent to two years without seeing a proper summer, without the sizzling heat that only exists outside Britain. Life – and a mostly active life – is decidedly too short for that, and there are not enough years as it is to properly see the whole world and its sights and people. My theory is not to let time go past without gazing at the wonders of the world: as some American person said to us, we only go round once. We do not have a repeat performance of our precious life on this earth.

However, after having had our third baby, it was a little difficult to go backpacking as he was still only seven or eight months of age when summertime came round again, and there were two older children to take into consideration. So we took a holiday to Brittany in Northern France mostly, with a little bit of Normandy where I am from thrown in, but with the car to make things easier that first year. The weather turned out to be rather capricious, which marred the beautiful Brittany coast. Any wonderful rugged cliff looks rather miserable under rainy, misty skies, although some people would argue it makes it more mysterious, and it can be transformed into an almost tropical postcard when the sun deigns to shower its glorious rays on it. The first week had glorious weather as we visited lovely old Dinard and its buildings with slate roofs, with the river meandering through it and the lovely romantic castle along the canal with the inviting barges. We visited a good friend of mine, Catherine, along the way as she lives in the pretty town of Rennes; some medieval towns and the prehistoric site of Carnac are the most famous attractions in the area. The water was omnipresent; the sea, rivers, and canals make Brittany a very pretty place despite the changing weather so typical of the area.

The *gites* – or bed and breakfast places – where we stayed were strategically situated, always in gorgeous areas and in beautiful buildings, and the breakfasts were typically Bretons and therefore delicious with pancakes, and special cakes from the area.

The prices were also reasonable and the rooms usually large enough to accommodate our large family; we had brought a transportable baby cot with us to allow us to book a place more easily. The advantage of having a car was that we could carry so much with us for once. We often had some walks through the pretty villages before setting off each day, and then suddenly the weather turned and unfortunately it rained and rained and rained to our disappointment.

It was a shame as we were about to visit Locronan, a very beautiful medieval town which is so well preserved, and it would have been better to see it under blue skies. These two pictures show the contrast in weather and the changing mood that pervaded us.

We then finished our Brittany trip going back to surprisingly sunny Normandy with the most impressive Mont St Michel, where our daughter put her foot in the moving sands that surround the mountain, which had been a great defence for years. It was a good way to finish the trip on a high note.

FROM SEATTLE TO THE ROCKIES AND DOWN TO SALT LAKE CITY

SUMMER 1995

The following year did not include a backpacking trip either due to other circumstances this time, and the chance to go back to the States thanks to my husband's conference in Seattle. We had decided we could not afford taking our now large family on such a holiday, so the two eldest children went off to Italy with their grandparents – at least they would have some sunshine – and we took Marc, the little one who was still under two years of age and therefore very low-cost to travel with, along with us; I mostly just had to pay for my flight. We first flew to Vancouver as this was cheaper, but it was a very long 20-hour trip, stopping over at Calgary, and then another nine hours during which our son hardly slept and kept fidgeting. He was quite happy but just slept for 20 minutes or so. We then took a shuttle bus, and I was desperate for a bed and sleep. At long last in Seattle, we managed to have some disturbed sleep as the buggy trick did not seem to be of any use this time. Luckily we had a huge breakfast at Pike Place Market with a view onto the sea and that gave us our energy back to do some sightseeing around Seattle, including The Dome, famous for baseball. We then went back to the hotel for the conference reception where we met some of my husband's colleagues. Our little son went from arms to arms, especially popular with the ladies, already a little charmer. We had three days in Seattle, and one of them we spent at the zoo with a friend of mine from Texas. It was really good to see her, and her children were good company for our son.

Then our proper holiday started and we hired a car to start our tour by going to the wonderful Rockies under sunny skies to start with – and then less so.

We bought a great baby seat for the car – since the car rental company had not provided one – from the Salvation Army; a very comfy seat for $4. We drove to Snoqualmie Falls with their beautiful alpine scenery and forested slopes, and had a lovely walk to the falls. We then found a beautiful hotel in Leavenworth, a picturesque town reconstituted in the Bavarian way with lovely buildings.

Then we met some South African people in the hotel who told us to stay with them when we were next going to be in Vancouver as this was now where they lived; this was most kind of them. After a stroll along the clear lake and in the lake itself, we drove on for quite a while before being able to find a decent hotel. The car was definitely an advantage to be able to cover the miles in order to find accommodation whenever necessary.

Then the weather turned, as it did on our previous trip in Brittany. Our accommodation for the next few nights in various places turned out to be lovely bed and breakfast places; one of them was lost in the deep dark forest where bears and even a cougar once ventured close to the place. We were now in truly Canadian scenery with beautiful waterfalls: Dawson Falls, Helmcken Falls ... some cutting into a canyon of red and volcanic rocks; we went to the top of the Green Mountains and had a view over thick forests and the wonderful wilderness of Canada.

Then we headed towards famous Jasper and we did not know where to look; the scenery was superb all around us as we were heading towards higher mountains and more peaks with snow on them. The sun shone again the next day, which was a bonus for the magnificent vistas we were to see from our superb Toyota. One mountain was dedicated to Terry Fox, a young man who ran across Canada with an artificial leg and raised a huge amount of money for a charity fighting bone cancer; sadly, he lost his fight at the young age of 22.

We soon had a wonderful sight in the shape of Mt Robson, the highest peak of the Canadian Rockies, with a strata of snow on its top. It was lovely to stretch our legs that day for a 4.5 km trek along the turquoise river in the woods leading to Kinney Lake. The walk was just wonderful and Marc was very happy in the backpack and loved to look at the water. I felt like I could go walking like this for days and camp in that glorious scenery with the river gurgling along, although the possibility of bears in the vicinity was perhaps daunting for camping. We then drove on through the national parks of Jasper and Banff with stupendous views everywhere; one vista after another of snowy peaks and lakes everywhere, and all these were glimmering in the sunshine.

These spectacular images were imprinted forever in our minds, and we were lucky enough to see some mountain goats and quite a few lovely chipmunks very close to us.

The next part of this long day trip saw us stopping at Athabasca Glacier where we did some walking and again the temptation to walk further was present, but we were ill-equipped for it and this was not a good idea with a baby.

We found that the 'info centres' were very good at giving us information on bed and breakfast places, which were usually nicely located and very pleasant.

The weather became worse again later on, and it was very rainy when we visited Moraine Lake and went on to Banff, which was a busy town with many interesting shops. We then went back towards the USA where we spent a night in Missoula on an Indian reservation.

There was a very interesting museum there dedicated to the Indians in the Black Foot area.

We were on the road again through the different rounded mountains of Montana, with the foothills of the Rocky Mountains never too far away. The wind had dropped by then and the sun started feeling much warmer at last, and we felt like Jack Kerouac reincarnated. You could now imagine the Far West; in fact, we reached what used to be a trail for the pioneers back in the 1860s, the Oregon Trail, where the Indians regularly attacked. En route, we visited the interesting frontier town of Butte. Around 300,000 people went on the trail and roughly a tenth died en route.

After many more miles, we reached the famous Yellowstone Park, but had to find accommodation quite a long way away as it was rather expensive to stay around the park. The entrance was pretty disappointing with many trees which had burnt and thus were in poor condition, but the park was dotted with some nice green valleys. We reached the Norms Geyser Basin – this was our first view of geysers and *fumaroles* – and finished this day trip at Mammoth with hot springs and beautiful white basins of mineral deposits. These deposits are caused by the evaporation of water, and with the beautiful mountain scenery, we were reminded somewhat of Cappadocia. The next day saw us coming back into the park in the direction of Old Faithful, probably the most famous of geysers; there were more bluish/white basins bubbling en route, and we became part of groups of tourists patiently waiting for Old Faithful to erupt high in the air, faithfully performing every seventy minutes for the joy of the tourists. Our son was most impressed by this amazing act of nature. We saw more geysers spurting up and down with rage, and we did not want to leave but had to, and were soon back on the road to Grand Teton Park with even more, different spectacular scenery.

Later on, the scenery transformed itself into plains surrounded by mountains, and forested slopes in canyons and drier mountains before we reached the outskirts of Salt Lake City, the furthest down we went on this trip. Salt Lake City spread for miles and miles, and some of the mountains we passed before reaching it had fires on them.

The temperature around SLC was hovering around 32 to 35 degrees. Our hotel was luckily not too far from the centre of the city, and we were able to reach it in fifteen minutes. We walked to the Mormon Temple area with a beautiful white church assembly room and glistening high-rises taking its reflection in the sunshine. Within the gardens were flowers and fountains; there were young girls of all nationalities called sister so and so, and a young Mormon guide took us around the temple and showed us a film about the Mormon religion, always with beautiful young people. One of the church's early leaders, Brigham Young, had 54 children in 16 families; now I am not saying that the Mormons are all polygamous, but it still exists.

The next drive for Allan was a very long one to Baker City, crossing Idaho – a mainly flat, arid, and uninteresting area. We reached Oregon and immediately the scenery became much more interesting, with mountains in soft waves on our horizon.

The next day, we actually crossed the 45th parallel, halfway between the Equator and the North Pole. Later on, we crossed Oregon and were back in Washington State, headed towards the Cascade Mountains covered with fir trees, and then we crossed the border again to get back to Canada.

We entered Vancouver with colourful skyscrapers towering in front of us, and parked somewhere in order to take the bus to the city centre. Canada Place, which is in a shape of a boat, was very good and so were the older Gasman quarters.

We were not too sure on the way back where we had parked our car, but my husband memorably remembered a place called 'Yip the tailor' and thus we were able to find the car!

We drove on to Abbotsford where the house of our hostess was (the people we had met at the beginning of our trip), as they had agreed to have us. The house was lovely and very comfortable, and we were delighted to stay with some people for a change. We mostly visited Stanley Park, a very enjoyable park with views of Vancouver, ponds and flowers, and full of black squirrels, where we were able to stroll in a more relaxed manner. In the evening we went to some restaurant in their huge van and had a good time, paying for their meal to thank them for their kindness. The next day was spent visiting the anthropological museum, which had an array of very interesting huge totems and exhibits from all around the world. We had covered 4,500 miles during our hectic trip when we said goodbye to our lovely faithful Toyota. We took a bus back to Vancouver from the car company to reach our YWCA, where we were to spend our last night; Marc was already missing his comfy seat.

This was a very fascinating trip, but quite a tiring and decidedly rushed one; but we had seen so much, and travelling by car was the most obvious thing to do in the States and Canada. This trip also showed that a holiday travelling miles and miles for days on end in a car could still be enjoyed by a young child. After the long flight and the first night during which he was rather restless, our little boy seemed to adapt to this travelling routine with happiness and ease, taking it all in, gazing from his window over the vast scenery or falling asleep during a good chunk of the travelling day, which made him rested and happy.

Italy: Firenze to South of Rome

SUMMER 1996

Backpacking was back on track with a trip on the hovercraft this time to leave a cold, typical grey-laden summer sky in Britain, and a long but enchanting trip on the train right down to Italy, sleeping in a couchette; this was more than half of the fun of that trip, and saved us five airline tickets to Italy, which would have cut dramatically into our budget at that time.

Do remember that travelling by train gives your children some price reductions – much more so than airlines – and this is something worth considering if your budget is fairly tight and your destination not so far away, especially if it is within Europe.

The sun was already beating down on us when we arrived in Italy and tiredness overcame me at first, but not our children nor my husband who were eagerly visiting the place while I rested for a while. Sudden heat can be quite tiring and oppressive at first, and what I would recommend if this happens to you or your children is to take it easy, look for some shade, and drink a lot of water, particularly if you are not used to the climate.

We visited some very touristy but gorgeous towns such as Firenze and its impressive Duomo and famous bridge, but it was a very busy town with every corner full of tourists from all over the world. Pisa, with its leaning tower actually in danger of leaning even more, felt quite romantic and its glittering white was unforgettable against the perfectly blue sky. What marred our Italian trip this time was the rather expensive cost of everything and, of course, when you have to multiply food by five, this was a problem we had not counted on. Travelling, though, was quite cheap.

On such holidays I found that going to some parks or even zoos gave the children and the adults a welcome break from monuments sightseeing and crowds of people, which can be overwhelming. Such places can be found everywhere in almost any town, and it is worth looking at your map of the town to discover where they are located, and how close they are to the museum, the cathedral, or the square with the monuments that you intend to visit.

It will also provide you with some shade; some peaceful respite from walking; a place to have your picnic; and basically a place where you are able to stop and re-assess whatever you need to re-assess in your life or on the trip itself, all the while giving the children a break from constant 'visiting' and some freedom to partake in more mundane activities such as feeding the ducks or having a good run round or whatever takes their fancy. The square or park is also a good place to stop and rest for a while rather than charging on, and it will make everyone appreciate their visit even more; the little pleasures of life are often the treasures of time to be remembered and cherished. Too often, people on packages do not have the time to rest wherever they want and have to follow the group.

We travelled by train on to the more southern parts of Italy and were relieved to note that prices went down from Rome onwards. So my next piece of advice is, if you are a bit short of money, head at once to the south in Italy; it was true then, and I am sure this is still the case nowadays. However, in Rome we walked past majestic buildings and down to the enchanting Trevi

Fountain where my husband and I had stopped years before, back later on with three kids in tow! The Coliseum and the Forum were a delight for the kids; they climbed on those well polished stones, quite used to the heat by now. I had forgotten how big and imposing the Coliseum was; it is unfortunate that it is getting damaged by pollution though. We then walked on through the majestic piazzas such as Navona, Rotonda ... and the Vatican in all its splendour. McDonald's was our saviour in Italy, being so much cheaper even though it was not typical Italian food, although there was actually delicious pasta dishes in all of them, something I have yet to experience in any other McDonald's around the world. It is usually not my favourite place, but it was cheaper!

After the grandeur of Rome, we took a train to Naples and another to Salerno, already down south quite a lot.

Salerno was a maze of medieval quarters with tiny, dark roads leading to the Duomo, which was very beautiful inside; fresh and painted white and very light with well preserved paintings. It also housed the tomb of one pope and a treasury shining in gold and silver in a beautifully adorned room downstairs, which also contained the remains of St. Matthew. We sat along the promenade in the evening in front of the sea savouring delicious ice cream; there were palm trees all along the promenade and we could see the Amalfi Coast in the background.

We woke up the next day to an incredible curtain of rain and lightning, and a sky totally grey covering the Amalfi Coast, which we found somewhat disappointing in itself because of the high number of houses that had sprung all over the mountainside, leaving no gap for the wilderness.

Still, it had allowed us a break on the coast after much city sightseeing and it can be a welcome break for the children and the adults, regardless of their love of sites. You do have to maintain the right balance between wanting to gorge yourself with site after site (a tendency I must admit I am guilty of) and the need to relax, stop for a bit, and take time to play in sand and sea – especially under the normally gorgeous azure Italian skies. They beat the greyish days of an English summer anytime. Besides, children as well as adults do need vitamin D from the sun, as long as there is no abuse of this double-edged life giver. I do strongly believe that children will benefit from proper sunshine abroad in order to be healthy and ready to face school and dreary days back in Britain. So do not be afraid to take your young children with you in the middle of summer. Many people are wary, but children can and do adapt to all sorts of weather conditions. If they are rather pale by nature as many English roses are, then they just need to take extra precautions. The human body is surely meant to resist 28 to 30 degree temperatures, and the southern countries tend to be most keen on children and often will shower you and your kids with kindness.

I have to say that the Italians seemed not as child-friendly as I remembered them; they have possibly become more self-centred and want to enjoy the more material things in life, and are thus having fewer children. This came as a surprise to me as Italy is a Catholic country renowned for its love of children.

Next on the itinerary was Pompeii; we spent a whole afternoon in this huge, wonderful, and quite eerie place. We saw some bodies from which they had made moulds, and we could still see their skulls covered in grey ashes.

Some roofs were still standing; whole streets were intact, as were some houses with mosaics and stairs still inside; there were temples that were very well preserved, and even a huge amphitheatre which would have been the equivalent of a leisure centre. This was quite an impressive sight with the now calm Vesuvius in the background. Then it was back to Salerno for the night and visit to Amalfi the next day, where we walked up the busy streets to where the lovely cathedral stood. But we thought it was rather a scrubby place and that it had lost its splendour.

However, it was good to go on the little pebbly beach below and have fun in the water.

Then it was time for more sightseeing, so we went by bus to Paestum, an archaeological site close to a beach. We were away from the crowds and packed houses at long last; this reminded us of Agrigento in Sicily where Allan and I had been before the children. We looked at the site and then went off to the beach, which was great! It was actually the hottest day so far!

Then it was time to get back up north and it was a long train journey back. The beaches that we could see from the train from Salerno to Naples looked rather filthy, and people were swimming among the rubbish; hopefully this area would have been cleaned by now. We stopped at Rome to catch the last train of the day to go to Orvieto, and there a funicular took us from the station to the town perched on a plateau. We were lucky to find an apartment with two bedrooms, quite a relative luxury! We walked to the beautifully adorned Duomo with paintings on the outside and sculpted figures describing different Christian scenes; the views to the valley and the mountains behind were beautiful, and the price of food was excellent! The next day, we took yet another train to Siena, where prices were inflated yet again because of mass tourism. We found accommodation with some difficulty in a convent from which we had a lovely view over the Duomo from our bedroom window, and then proceeded to visit the beautiful medieval place – not surprisingly full of tourists. Lastly, we headed back to Florence for some last-minute sightseeing and then took to our 'sleepers' on the train for the long journey back to Paris. From Paris, our last leg had us changing stations to go from Gare du Nord to the boat, and then the hovercraft again to the UK – and back to grey skies. But we had a few days left which we spent in Newport with Allan's parents, which was a nice end to the holiday.

Corsica

AUGUST 1998

This trip was minus our oldest this time round as he did not seem too keen; teenage time was coming and he went to stay with my brother in France instead. In order to ensure a cheaper trip, since we had travelled quite a lot that year, we decided to take the train once again, and then the boat to Corsica. For a long time I had wanted to visit this island called île de beauté in France, and its name was certainly deserved. This trip required some organisation as it was rather difficult – actually almost impossible – to obtain boat information from France, although the Internet would have helped and nowadays this would not be a problem at all. I had to enquire through companies in France and ask them to send me the relevant details and book through them, ensuring this would coincide with our trip – not such an easy feat. We were to see the most glorious mountain scenery along fantastic 'blonde' beaches and small cities crowned by ochre citadels, changing colour according to the time of the day and the slanting rays of the sun, were just fascinating in and of themselves.

When we arrived in Nice in the south of France, the weather was grey and disappointing, and quite cold as well, but this changed as soon as we arrived in Corsica. We arrived in l'Ile Rousse on the boat and took a taxi across superb mountains in the night – promising some wonderful scenery. The hotel I had booked was a very nice one and the first day was spent relaxing on the very pretty beach; this was a good start apart from the fact that Vivienne, our daughter, had forgotten her bucket, spades, and buoy in the car of a lady who had been nice enough to take us back up to the hotel!

We then took a train to Calvi; little villages were dotted here and there along the way and the sun was shining brightly – in fact, it was becoming pretty hot. We stayed in a youth hostel and visited the old town with its pedestrian streets under a majestic citadel on a peninsula, and a beautiful pink church sitting in the middle of a pretty old square in the lovely shade. After the visit, we spent some time on the beach in the bay. Along the beach – or rather above it – the famous legionnaires were parachuting, which was quite a spectacle, with many rounded shapes floating eerily above us. The next day saw us taking a small train to Lumio, where we tried to find the beach and were helped by these very legionnaires in their impeccably white uniforms. Eventually we could not carry on, meeting a wall of rocks on our way to the beach, and we had to take a train back to Calvi.

Yachts were everywhere as we were wandering the streets at night and they added to the luminosity of the scenery, so I wore the only smart dress I had to match the occasion – the little black dress which is apparently in every woman's wardrobe, even though I do not particularly enjoy to dress up; however, it just seemed right and it was probably one of the last times I wore it.

Another day, we walked uphill from the beautiful bay of Porto, where we stayed for a couple of nights. We had reached Porto by bus via small mountain roads with houses perilously clinging to the sharp edged mountains; it was so peaceful that we ended up soaking ourselves in incredibly warm rivers.

In fairly hot climates, it is always worth considering a trip with children that involves some bathing, and therefore some cooling down. It helps to keep tempers calm and provides a respite from the sometimes hot, sweaty walks up mountain paths. In another instance, we walked from a little town called Piana along the road to the *calanques* – reddish formations of mountains perched high above the sea. This was a superb walk but we had to be careful of the many cars passing by us, luckily driving very slowly to admire the *calanques*. We then took a bus to Ajaccio, which had more beautiful scenery. Afterwards, we had another walk around the market and the old Ajaccio and, of course, more beach time (it is an island after all) and as usual we had some wonderful French food: baguettes, *viennoises*, and chocolate.

Then it was on to more ordinary Propriano, but the mountain and beaches were spectacular. Beaches are everywhere and most beautiful in Corsica, with fine golden sand and the bluest of seas; its most beautiful side is the west which will delight children and adults alike with an array of beaches and sightseeing – indeed, you are never too far from beaches..

Another bus took us to Sartène, a pretty town perched on a mountain away from the sea this time. Within its entanglement of narrow medieval streets and imposing houses – where our children had fun going up and down the many steps – the place appealed to their natural curiosity and also provided some shade in the middle of the day. Corsica gets hot but never really too hot thanks to the sea breezes gently blowing. Then it was back to the beach in Propriano in the afternoon.

We pursued our route down the west coast, again by bus, and by this time the drivers had started knowing who we were and were very friendly. Although it had rained that morning, we arrived under lovely sunshine. Bonifacio is incredible with its houses literally perched on the cliffs. A wonderful way to see this phenomenon was to view it from the sea, again a plus with children, circling this wonderful place and entering pirate caves under its rocks.

Of course, we also visited the site where Napoleon Bonaparte had stayed, but unfortunately could not look inside, yet there were superb views onto the limestone cliffs and views on the other, wilder side onto the precipice below. We hitchhiked with a person from Brittany who had left his family at the camping ground and were deposited by the pretty St Julia beach near Porto Vecchio. The beach was like a lagoon with a tropic-like sea, so clear and so warm, and we took advantage of this idyllic beach to have fun in the sea and sunbake in the sunshine before returning to our lovely white bedroom in the hotel.

We got back to Ajaccio with a more threatening and darkening sky and a bus trip which made everyone on board feel somewhat nauseous and quite pleased to finally get off.

We went for a walk along the harbour which was full of huge boats, including a superb cruising boat, and then it started raining, so we went back to our hotel for a restless night due to the stormy weather out there.

We had to get up early – not long after we had finally settled down to sleep – in order to catch the little train from Ajaccio, which travelled three and a half hours through mountains and forests to arrive at a windy and stormy Bastia. We visited the very picturesque town during terrible wind gusts, spoiling some of the beauty of the place, and managed to find a sheltered spot to have a picnic overlooking the harbour with our little boy singing happily at the top of his voice for every passer-by. We went to see where our boat – which was going to take us back to the mainland – was, but it was not there yet because of the storm.

We left at 3 am instead of 11 pm on the huge boat simply called Le Corse, and settled in our sleeping berths. Although the sea was very rough, the tablets we had taken must have helped because we really slept pretty well until 9 am; the boat arrived an hour later under sunshine and the wind had gone. Booking sleeping berths on long crossings was certainly worth considering with children; it helped avoiding sea sickness and permitted a good rest which reclinable seats would never have really provided.

We left our luggage at the hotel we had booked in Nice and went on to visit the pretty Italian-like town of Menton. The beach there though was pebbly and disappointing after the beautiful, sandy Corsican beaches. The next day, we learnt about Princess Diana's death in Paris on my birthday – what a tragic ending. Strangely enough, she had spent some time in Corsica on some yacht – maybe one of those yachts we were admiring from the harbour – and we were going to be in Paris soon afterwards, following in her footsteps. Coming back to a happier note, Corsica was a very beautiful island indeed and well deserves its nickname of île de Beauté.

The Peloponnese, Greece

SUMMER 1998

All five of us were back for this trip to Greece, which concentrated mostly on the Peloponnese area where most of the ancient ruins are to be found. It was quite emotional to come back to Athens with three children this time, each head forming a pyramid shape next to each other: they grow so quickly! It had been thirteen years! My advice once more is to take children on holidays with you right from when they are fairly small as time goes by so fast, and we sensed that this might be one of the last holidays with our eldest; sadly, eventually they want to travel under their own wind. This was actually my third visit to Athens personally; the 2,500 year old Acropolis had not lost its grandeur, the sky was as blue as ever, and there was a gentle wind blowing which kept the temperature mild. There were water fountains everywhere – a great idea which helped us all along as we walked through the ruins and also through the beautiful and oldest part of Athens outside the ruins, the Plaka. Our little boy had a good hour's sleep by the cathedral, quite shattered after his long day's walk.

Then we were en route to the canal of Corinth, a low, long stretch of azure water gleaming below us and perpendicular white cliffs above, with little boats gently floating along – a rather lovely introduction to the Peloponnese.

We found accommodation in nearby Loutraki, a beautiful spa town with clean white and fairly modern buildings. We had a brief walk around and a picnic on its nice pebbly beach backed by mountains, then walked to the spa area, close to some waterfall with palm trees lining the promenade.

We were thinking of taking the bus back to old Korinthos, but it was quite awkward and would have required three buses, so when a family from Belgium offered to take us there in their Renault Espace, we did not hesitate. We visited the ruins of Corinth, which had been devastated in part by many an earthquake; the ancient city was, at some point, bigger than Athens! The Temple of Apollo was still standing with seven columns intact, and the ancient water sources were still supplying the new Corinth with water; there was also a good museum with some pieces dating back to 1,300 BC! It was quite moving to visit Corinth and remember learning in church about Peter talking to the Corinthians to convert them to a more gentile way of life. The heat during the visit was quite overwhelming to start with, and we were soon looking for shade.

We visited the nearby pretty town of Nafplion – where there were more tourists to be seen and thus increased prices generally – and walked up the 900 steps to the fort; an exhausting trek for the older ones but just a jaunt for the younger ones. This showed us once more that we must travel when we are fit and not wait for the children to get older because by then, unfortunately, we are older ourselves and time is of the essence. The panorama was very beautiful and it was worth the sweaty trek. In the evening after having been in the water among rocks, we had a gentler walk to see the castle 'in' the water. The sunsets over the bay on the promenade back from the beach provided golden rays bejewelling the sea with a mysterious aura – simply wonderful.

We then took a bus to Epidaure with its superb theatre and other ruins, the names of all these places coming back to me from my book of Greek myths and becoming a reality: this was the ancient pharmaceutical centre of the antiquity.

After the visit we hired a taxi to take us to a sandy beach not far away where the children had a lot of fun, even the older one. However our eldest, Jim, got stung, possibly by a jelly fish, and the return walk along the lovely path in the wilderness among the cliffs reminding us of Corsica was a bit sore for him.

Yet another bus the next day took us to Mycenes; the bus was full of French kids and their supervisor, and their trip was being subsidised by the Credit Lyonnais at a very decent price: they were lucky children. We climbed to the *citadelle* among slippery rocks to reach the famous lion door, dating back 3,000 years, with the dry hills in the background. The site itself is beautifully situated with sheer mountains around it, but it was somewhat disappointing as it was left as a maze of fallen rocks, which dominated the plain below. It would have been so much more impressive if the Greeks had tried to restore its grandeur rather than leaving it half abandoned. We next visited the tomb of Agamemnon and Clytemnestra who had him killed by her lover who became king of Mycenae and who in turn was killed by Agamemnon and Clytemnestra's son in revenge. We went on to the beach later on for some respite from sightseeing, and a stroll through the village of Mycenes for some treats.

Another day had us in Argos, a little place not so well known and not so touristy, with a beach and a lovely harbour. This was followed the next day by a very early start (5 am) to catch the bus to Kosmos through beautiful scenery with arid mountains. This was quite a surprise due, I suppose, to the altitude and the trees which were mostly plane trees – northern trees I did not expect to see here.

There were splendid views to be had from up there before going back down in the back of a pickup truck, seeing as there was no public transport to drop us where we wanted. The wind was blowing our hair in a delightful way, and the warmth welcomed us back as we descended the mountains; it had been quite an exhilarating drive.

The heat had come back as we were waiting for the bus to Sparta; in front of us the plain was stretched out, with olive trees and the mountains in the background. After quite a long wait, the bus arrived to our exhausted relief. We managed to find a decent hotel with a swimming pool. Sparta was a gruelling place which deserved its name, as the heat was indeed oppressive and you could imagine why the Spartans were what they were just from this 'squashing' heat, which wrapped itself around your legs just like in Texas. We visited the few ruins which were left before freshening up in the delightful swimming pool, and my husband and I actually went for an evening walk, just the two of us, while our eldest was babysitting.

Mystras, the Byzantine city that we next visited, was quite a different place with very well preserved beautiful red-roofed basilicas appearing here and there among lovely trees that provided us with some shade. Our daughter Vivienne was taking endless notes of the sites, drawing pictures of ruin after ruin, asking about the history of the various places, and she was only about nine. This was a pleasure to see and it again showed us how a young child will be influenced by visiting places and develop a keener interest in what happens worldwide. We imagined her as a future archaeologist. Then it was back to the hotel in Sparta, and back for another swim at night and the next morning before catching the bus to incredible Monemvasia, with its huge rock jutting out on the end of the pier revealing, tucked behind this massive fortress-like rock, a maze of old Byzantine houses – a totally delightful spectacle. We ended up in a lovely room with a kitchenette – a nice change from the usual hotel rooms - which allowed us to do some cooking for once. We had soup, spaghetti in tomato sauce with salami, and some watermelon for dessert, all cooked and served by Allan – a very nice treat indeed! The owners had given us the fruit and kept on giving us bags of juicy fruit. This was a nice respite from eating out, giving us a break from restaurants and saving us money, too.

After a lovely breakfast of oranges (provided by our hosts) which made some delicious orange juice squeezed by our son Jim, bread with butter and jam, cakes, tea, coffee, and milk, we were ready to face the next day.

After starting with the pebbly beach below where we got slightly sunburnt, we visited the old and picturesque town of Monemvasia with its ramparts looking onto the sea, some stone houses, and a long 2 km causeway that took us to the old town with a castle dominating the whole place.

This was quite an unforgettable destination, and I am surprised this has remained not widely known even to this day. The next day was spent relaxing on the beach at Pori near the town of Monemvasia, and we found a little pool by the rocks close to the sandy beach which was not very accessible for swimming.

We left Monemvasia to reach a different type of place altogether in the Mani, which was famous for its former military base and where neighbours, in ancient times, warred upon each other. Weapons were still being sold in the shops, a remnant of an aggressive time. The atmosphere of this very military-esque place could still be felt in its harsh architecture with severe, square fortress-like buildings and the countryside dotted here and there with rocky walls. We stayed in a place called Aeropoli; the weather was getting very heavy, although it freshened in the evening and even rained, but the room in the tavern where we stayed was quite hot. We went to some caves, but only the children went in as it was quite expensive; then we went to the beach below which had big pebbles, but still the water was lovely. After a while, I was able to find a little church where I read in the shade of a palm tree. It was a nice relaxing day in the imposing, moody Mani. Methoni citadel, further on in our tour of the Peloponnese, felt like a remnant of the Mani, though in a more romantic way, possibly due to its lovely seaside setting, where you could swim in delicious warm waters under the imposing ruins.

The sandy beach flanked by the huge fortress was probably the nicest one of this trip and shallow enough for weak swimmers like me. We visited the fortress in the late afternoon, and it was quite grandiose. Next on our itinerary was Pyrgos with a much more ordinary beach before going on to Olympia which, of course, had to be on our itinerary. There, we ran in the gruelling heat of the stadium and Jim was the winner to Allan's dismay – a sign of times. Even our little one enjoyed his run and will be able to boast in the future that he ran in this most celebrated of stadiums where the real Olympics had originated. After that we all moved pretty slowly as the heat was not abating. We also visited the super museum with bronze art and statues that were 2,500 years old.

We then left the wonderful Peloponnese at Patras for a last visit in Delphi, with its gorgeous mountain scenery including temples dotted here and there.

We found a beautiful large hotel room at a very decent price (30 pounds) with a beautiful oak ceiling, two large beds and a third smaller one, a beautiful tiled floor, a gorgeous bathroom, and a superb view onto the mountains!

We got up the next day with a view onto the mountains on one side and the sea on the other side, and sheep with their little bells passing through between. We then went on to visit the site after having done the necessary shopping; the columns, theatre, Temple of Apollo where the famous Oracle of Delphi had been housed, then on to the Athena temple where Marc fell asleep in the shade of a tree. The children enjoyed walking up and down the paths, feeling the heat less than the adults; they were more resilient to the effects of heat and their excitement made them forget about their tiredness, that is after Marc had woken up. To see their pleasure was in itself a source of pleasure for us, the parents, for years to come.

Then it was back to Athens and the UK: we were allowed to go in the cockpit where we could have a great view above the clouds, something that sadly would not be allowed nowadays. This was a good family holiday away from the daily routine with souvenirs of wonderful ruins sometimes in need of being taken care of, and superb scenery which included forested and 'bald' mountains, and skies and seas so blue and so limpid.

Dordogne, France

SUMMER 1999

The next trip was an overland trip by car through some part of France to reach the Dordogne area, to stay at the place of a mature student of mine.

This was not a backpacking trek, but it is worth mentioning for its variety and the fact that it displays some areas of France where I come from; so there will be just a few words with quite a few photographs to describe this trip.

First of all, we stopped in Normandy – in Flers, the town I come from – to visit my parents. Then it was onward further south to LeMans with the beautiful old town, Tours, where I studied and a visit to some of the nearby castles including Saumur and Chambord.

We drove further down near Poitiers to visit the famous Futuroscope, a very interesting theme park, and had a great day there, adults and children alike.

Then it was off to St Emilion, a 'kingdom' of wine before reaching my student's house near Duras in the Dordogne area.

This was the real south of France, starting with the lovely red tile roofs that I love in villages perched on the hills; the wonderful fields of sunflowers; and the gorgeous converted barn in the middle of nowhere. The house inside was beautifully done with huge rooms where they had preserved as much of the character of the house as possible. It was very welcoming, and we were very lucky to be able to rent such a place for such a small sum of money – around 100 pounds for a week, or even ten days if we had wanted. We had the pleasure of living in the place without the hassle of doing work on it.

We set out from our great base visiting some more castles such as Bergerac and Beynac Castle, perched on the top of the hill overlooking the river, and the town of La Roque Gageac with more limestone cliffs standing out against the blue sky and picturesque houses lined along the river.

The weather was pretty hot and there were some thunderstorms in the evening – one very fierce one as we were coming back from Bergerac when a big branch hit the windscreen and we were lucky that nothing bad happened. It was pretty scary and the visibility was almost nil with very heavy rain; we felt so happy when we saw a McDonald's, the first time I have ever felt so pleased to see that place, as it meant we could stop for a while, and we were not far from our destination.

Later, the whole family except me (I had to finish some studying for my master's degree) went for a cool swim in the lake not so far from the house. We also did some canoeing on the Dordogne; this was a great activity and experience on the calm waters of the long, tortuous river.

We left our lovely place with a hint of sadness and went back up country, stopping over in famous Rocamadour, 'the citadel of faith', still in the Dordogne valley. Rocamadour, with its medieval streets and basilica, seemed to be hanging over a cliff.

It has been a place of pilgrimage since the twelfth century, and has been visited by kings and queens of France, Spain, and England who come to revere the Black Virgin (Madonna) and the tomb of St Amadour.

Then, we were on our way back towards the north, stopping near le Puy Du Fou in Brittany, where we experienced the company of hundreds of goats on the farm where we had been staying for a night; everyone was delighted to be among those friendly animals. Further onwards in Brittany, we experienced the eclipse of the sun and we stopped and visited with some English friends who were staying there; this was followed by a visit to a French friend whom I met years before when I spent a year in Cardiff all those years ago in order to improve my English. This was a lovely way to finish this great trip through a good part of western France.

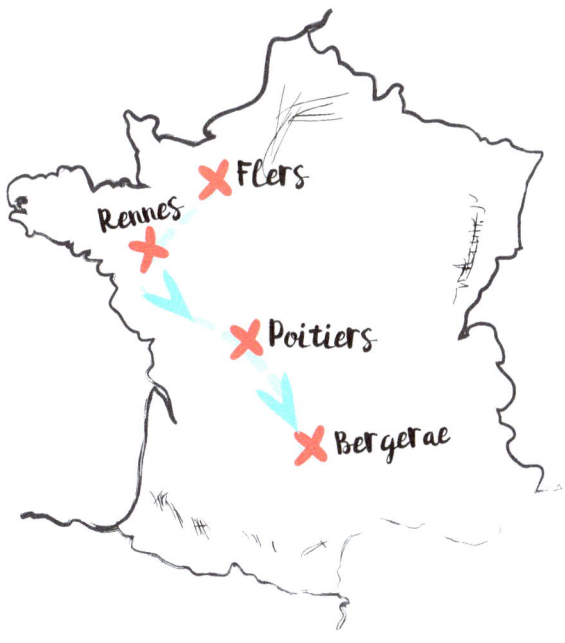

Taiwan

SUMMER 2000

My husband had some work to do in Taiwan for four weeks, so we thought we might as well extend this to a holiday around the island and joined him after two weeks. The flight took longer than expected; we changed planes at the modern, jewel-like Abu Dhabi airport, then again at Bangkok, where me missed the plane due to a delay in Abu Dhabi, and thus arrived much later than expected in Taipei where, luckily, we were expected. People were surprised to see our little family taking these planes to go that far while we were patiently waiting at the airport between planes.

The next day, we were pretty exhausted and slept in until quite late, then had a walk in a little park, crossing streets full of scooters often with three people on board.

The heat was quite intense and we returned soon after for a rest. Later on, we had our first experience of the grand Chinese buildings, beginning with Chiang Kai Shek Memorial Hall with its magnificent gate opening to a sort of temple flanked by two others. Strangely enough, loud pop music was blaring from loudspeakers while the other side was a much more tranquil picture, with tai-chi exercises that Vivienne and I joined. The temple was a grandiose sight to behold.

The next day, we went back to Chiang Kai Shek Memorial Hall and had a closer look inside where we saw his statue and two soldiers standing incredibly immobile, looking more like statues themselves than living men.

Next, we moved on to Peace Park, a pleasant place with pagodas and ponds. We spent the next two weeks in and around Taipei while Allan was working, and were at times invited in the evening with his work colleagues to enjoy some of the most delicious meals, which would make even the French envious – and I should know: apart from the odd salted pineapple, beware children!

We visited many temples sporting a riot of colours, full of people praying to the gods, and offering fruit and food to them. But let's go back to the weekend which we had with Allan before he started work again.

After a good night's sleep in the flat allocated to us, we took the underground to Beitou (I have to add that Marc was wonderful with the tube, knowing where we had to change, and that at such a young age) and arrived at some hot springs smelling of sulphur where a man was actually cooking his eggs – but then had the instrument he used to reach for the eggs confiscated from him. The next day was spent going to Sun Yat-sen Memorial Hall which contained memorabilia from the past, spreading the biased word of the 1912 Communist Revolution; then on to the City Hall before visiting Sogo, a huge department store full of Americans. The next day, we were invited to visit the zoo with Ming's wife; Ming was a colleague and ex-student of Allan's in the UK. We had a great day at the huge zoo under 36 degree temperatures and very little shade, but the children did not seem to mind and did not want to miss anything. We ensured that we had enough water with us so as not to get dehydrated.

We visited many colourful temples, full of people praying to the gods and laying out offerings, and had another evening of gorging ourselves with more delicious food including some shark soup (which I feel guilty about now); shrimp in some ball shapes encrusted with almonds; fish of all shapes including lobster; fruit such as mangoes, guavas, and pineapples – all so beautifully presented, and quite a different type of meal from our usual backpacking ones. This was not paid for by us and that probably explained it, as it would have been quite costly; I presume the university paid.

On another day, we went to the coast, which was not as interesting and somewhat dirty, but the children enjoyed themselves on the windswept beach. It was nice to be close to the sea rather than be surrounded by a sea of buildings for a change.

We had a very interesting day at the National Palace Museum which housed Chinese treasures imported from mainland China; just as well probably as they would most certainly have been lost or destroyed in the Cultural Revolution there. It was a very rainy day, so a good day for museums. The museum encompassed three storeys devoted to bronze, jade, and calligraphy, some objects being as old as 6,000 years! The huge number of pieces that we saw only represented 1% of all the Chinese treasures, and this was quite incredible! Then we took a bus to Lungshan Temple – which we had seen previously – to show Allan, who was quite impressed; it was all beautifully illuminated.

There were less pleasant visits to be had later on, including one to 'Snake Alley', where live snakes, small turtles, lemur-like animals, and beautiful fish were probably going to end up on someone's plate.

Taipei abounds with luxuriant parks full of inviting paths mysteriously taking you to waterfalls, ponds with lilies, turtles, and gorgeous little bridges straight from fairy tales in a forested environment; this was a real playground for the children. Taipei and its surroundings kept us busy for two weeks; we learnt a few Mandarin words, took the very efficient underground system every day, and had many smiles and hellos thrown at us, as we were obviously quite noticeable in this sea of Chinese people in an island which was at that time fairly un-touristy. We were met with a lot of kindness and generosity all along our holiday. We also visited the art museum, which was full of paintings and photos of the world and quite a few strange things as well, such as dresses with bulbs which lit up, metal sounding like a heartbeat, etc. We walked to Lin An-Tai Homestead, a beautiful traditional home and the oldest in Taipei, which consisted of a long house with a middle courtyard and sleeping accommodation, plus a lounge and a study; the middle being reserved for the parents and the sides, with other courtyards, for the sons – all gracefully adorned with lovely wooden carvings and furniture.

One of our last trips around Taipei was to go to Keelung by bus where we saw a huge white statue flanked by two huge yellow lions and more little statues, all this overlooking the sea: the whole sight was quite impressive and we went inside the statue and had a quick picnic in a concrete lotus flower giving onto this huge statue.

Before leaving Taipei, Yu-Chen, my husband's colleague, and her husband took us in their van to visit ceramic factories.

Her uncle had his own company there in Chungli and we came out with a few ceramic pieces, the children were spoilt and received a few presents, and there was drink and food galore.

We learnt that her husband had been the actual President's neighbour when he was little, and that we might even visit the President's house or his mother's in Tainan, when we reach this old capital where we would meet up again with this kind couple at the end of our trip. We went to a teahouse in the mountains in the evening, visiting on the way two superb temples perched over the hills and listening to the very unusual metallic sound of the Taiwanese forest, which I have never heard since anywhere else.

This picture is of a fruit market which we visited with our hosts; there were all sorts of fruit, including star fruit, mangoes, pineapples, and many fruits I had not heard of. It was quite a fascinating sight in and of itself.

Below is one of the colourful temples that we were going to see all along our trip around Taiwan (formerly Formosa, which means beautiful in Portuguese).

Taiwan is truly a beautiful island not just for its many rich temples and wonderful food, but also for its gorgeous scenery.

When my husband had finished his month's job, we said goodbye to our little flat, and took the tube and the train for Sao where we looked for hotels. By chance we met a pretty young Chinese woman who spoke English and took us in her car to look for hotels, which were quite expensive for Taiwan, and she eventually invited us to stay in her place instead, which we gratefully accepted.

Her house was beautiful and modern, decorated with graceful taste, and our bedrooms were just wonderful on two levels.

This made a change from our rather barren, cockroach-infested flat in Taipei. After a nice meal of noodles and fish, she took us to the lovely Nanfang'ao harbour, facing the Pacific. We walked through the various markets with her Filipino maid and ate sausages and chips as the eyes of the fish looking at us in various fish places made the children and myself feel a bit queasy, then we had a chat back at her house with her husband. Her English name was Angel – quite an appropriate name!

The next day, Angel drove us to the International Dance Festival in the park, and all her family was there. In this magical park, we discovered swimming-pools and lots of water areas, and wished we had taken our swimsuits with us. Luckily, it was all sorted out and I borrowed Angel's, so we managed to go under the waterfalls and watch the wonderful dances from all over the world: Paraguay with the lady graciously holding a jug over her head and dancing; China; Israel; Russia; and Ivory Coast. We missed some but were lucky enough and the whole spectacle was simply magical, topped off by a disco dance below illuminated water. This was a beautiful, unforgettable day thanks to our 'angel'. She took us the following day to visit her noodle factory, and then we had to reluctantly leave our gracious host – such kindness we had not seen since Turkey.

We then took the train towards the magnificent Taroko Gorge, which reminded us of Corsica, but with a different type of vegetation. We had a lovely walk towards the pagoda and the temple, crossing a suspended bridge above a turquoise river amid the beautiful framing mountains. The next day, we woke up to a perfect blue sky sharply defining the mountains; the scenery was truly spectacular. At the end of a walk, we arrived at the Wenshan hot springs where you could smell the sulphur. Some people were bathing in the hot water but we sort of had half of our bodies in cold water and half in hot water; it felt wonderful and refreshing after and before walking again in this tranquil area.

What magnificent vistas of waterfalls over more turquoise water seething in bubbling circles, and the dangerous beauty of the rocks below!

We read in the paper that Hualien, where we expected to go the next day, was threatened with an imminent earthquake. Nevertheless, we took the bus to Hualien where many army planes were hovering above; was it against some Chinese activity? Then we took a three hour train to Taitung without feeling any earthquakes, and we could see some rice plantations on the fertile plains below the mountains.

At our destination, the natives definitely had a browner complexion, more like Tahitians. The following day welcomed us with thunder and it felt quite miserable, so we headed for Shanyuan Beach, a lovely beach flanked by a mountainous backdrop. The sky was rather menacing though, so we had a quick picnic and a rest before walking to a temple along the beach, then quickly taxied back to damp Taitung. We went the next day to some beautiful gorge and river, and were able to swim and paddle in the water in quite an idyllic spot; we found ourselves with our own private beach/river in tranquil beauty. On the way back, our daughter noticed a green snake (flashback of Turkey here) which was actually a venomous bamboo snake zigzagging along. I must say we ran away from this fearsome creature, and had to have a drink to recover from this chilling encounter.

Kenting, our next port of call, was rather grey and rainy but we managed to have a picnic on a beach and, from time to time, the sun let a few rays out to warm our bodies. This was a very busy place.

We visited a typical Chinese house with red tiles and central yards; this type of very picturesque house has become quite a rarity now, many having been bulldozed to make room for high-rises and flats, which take up less room in an overcrowded island. This was supposed to be the Taiwanese Hawaii, and it started pouring down. Having said that, the next day we would suffer from the heat and it would be our own fault.

It was a bright and hot day and we spent most of it on the beach; the sun was strong and we went in the sea a lot. Clouds were bubbling up every so often and so we felt protected, but this was a big mistake. As we were returning to our hotel, we realised that all of us we were very red and I at once put large quantities of calamine on us, but we were soon hurting and our skin felt tight and uncomfortable. One lesson from this was that, never mind the clouds and the time spent in the sea, none of it will protect you, and you do get burnt in the water, something I had not realised. I felt guilty about not having protected the children enough from what was, after all, subtropical heat.

A mistake to avoid at all costs! In the evening, we still managed to catch a bus to Oluanpi, a coral garden which was unfortunately closed, but nevertheless in a wonderful park with superb views of the sea with a mountainous background where we had a pleasant walk under a labyrinth of plants.

After a bad night due to our sunburns, we had a day's travelling to Tainan where we were to meet Yu-Chen and her family once again.

The next day, we visited Chihkan Tower, a fort built by the Dutch in 1653. The Dutch have been everywhere, and on many trips we saw these forts and ramparts, etc. We visited more temples as Tainan was, after all, the old capital of the island and full of massive temples. We also went to the village where Yu-Chen's husband had spent his childhood. There were a lot of orchards growing in this area; some sort of ninja-chestnuts which grew in water abounded; rice fields; dragon eyes which looked like grapes; and sugar cane that we tasted on the spot. In the village, we met the President's mother and had a couple of pictures with her in front of her house, one of those typical red-roofed ones.

Our generous guides took us in their car to some huge temples that we had not seen before. We did not stop eating in the car: papayas, pineapple, bananas, cakes, tofu, yoghurts, peanut bars, and juice and water in quantity. We saw hell and heaven inside a dragon in yet another huge temple. People apparently donate a lot of money, hence the competition between these temples to be bigger than the others; we certainly had our fill of temples!

On our own again, we visited Chung Cheng University, said to be of an unusual architecture with a pond and black swans; it made us wonder why British universities in the majority do not build on that scale. Then by bus onto Alishan, a forested village perched up in the mountains at 2,000 meters altitude. The pineapple and banana trees gave way to high pine trees, and the hot subtropical climate to a fresh, temperate one; we felt cold and actually had to put our jumpers on for the first time. We found a superb room with shell pictures, reminding us of the sea in this alpine locale – all at a very decent price. Then we went for a walk along wooden paths in forests of very old, huge trees (some apparently as much as 2,000 years old) where Buddhist nuns were praying and singing.

At the end of the day, we waited to look at the sunset with the clouds below, like a sea of cream slightly draped in a pinkish light.

We left Alishan the next day in the rain, having been lucky the previous day; a typhoon had been spotted since we had arrived in Alishan and was announced in Taipei just as we arrived, ready to leave Taiwan a couple of days later.

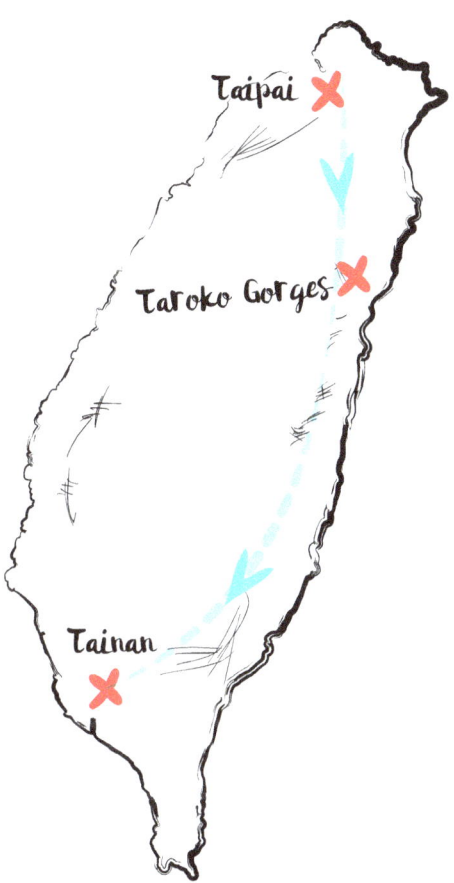

We were back in our flat and had quite a ferocious night, with the wind howling at high speed, rattling the windows of the flat and accompanied by a small earthquake – all in all quite an experience! The next day, we had a last walk to Chiang Kai Shek Memorial Hall but everything was closed due to the typhoon; its destruction was evident with various damaged objects strewn all over the place, after having fallen overnight. This was a sad Taipei under grey skies.

On the last day, we walked in the rain up to Sanyo Tower to see the whole of Taipei before meeting 'good old' Ming, who had been one of Allan's students, and quite a character!

The next morning, things were back to normal and we could leave for our next destination, two and a half days in Hong Kong before returning to the UK. So, we had to regretfully leave our beautiful island first thing in the morning to catch a taxi to the airport.

Hong Kong

2000

In Hong Kong, we took an ultra-modern train from the airport to Kowloon, and then a shuttle to some big expensive hotel where we could not really afford to stay. So while husband and son stayed with the luggage, my daughter and I looked for cheaper guesthouses. We found some sordid lift which took us to some old rickety place; strange and frightening-looking people of all races squeezed in the lift with us. No, we were not going to stay in such a shabby looking place where drugs seemed part of the whole thing, and where privacy hardly seemed to exist. We eventually found one place, rather pricier than in Taiwan but a lot safer than the previously visited ones. We proceeded to have a look at the port dominated by a sea of huge skyscrapers hiding the mountains behind. I was fairly disappointed whereas my husband and son enjoyed that view of the concrete jungle.

I think that must be a masculine thing. To me, high-rises are high-rises; they could be anywhere in the world, and they tend to hide the beauty of the landscape and also the sunlight.

The next day, we took the ferry and the tram to the famous Peak, and it seemed as if all these towers were going to fall on us along the way. At long last we could have a walk under some trees next to some great big houses, and contemplate the view over Hong Kong. We also had a wonderful walk in the park inside an aviary in deep vegetation which could almost make you forget that you were in a big metropolis. We also wandered through the other side of Hong Kong, contrasting with the ultra-modern: narrow streets of old traditional China tucked away behind huge glass walls, with markets selling their wares as they have for hundreds of years.

The following day welcomed us with thunderstorms and big yellow zigzags lighting up the sky; we had to find shelter before resuming our visit to the village of Stanley, where there were enticing caves of yellow sand for the children if the weather had been more pleasant. But the sky remained decidedly English with laden clouds and, indeed, the place was full of British people, so we just visited the covered markets looking for jade and nearly bought a big jade galleon. Instead we settled for a more modest jade dragon before catching the bus back to Aberdeen, with its sampans taking tourists for a ride on the waters. Here we had a last look at the waterfront in Kowloon with the Hong Kong skyscrapers on the other side before heading back for our last night in enchanting Southeast Asia.

Puglia, Italy

SUMMER 2001

On our next holiday, we went back to Europe with our two younger children, although my husband and I had a ten-day break (and conference for Allan) to Singapore and Kuala Lumpur sometime before that. Ever tempting Italy called to us again with all its history, narrow medieval streets, and its mostly glorious sunshine. We were off to Puglia this time, a region of southeast Italy comprising the boot which sees decidedly fewer tourists (outside Italian natives from other regions) and saw us arriving by train from Rome after a very cheap flight there from London. It felt strange to be back in Rome where we had been with our three children before, and quite nostalgic.

From there, we took a five and a half hour train to Bari which revealed itself to be more expensive than we thought; we had planned on southern Italy being more reasonable after the last trip to the expensive northern parts. We had a glimpse of the old city, a maze of cobbled narrow streets so typical of Italy, with clothes hanging overhead, lending it a very homely atmosphere. The town was alive with many crafts such as pasta-making outside on the street – a family venture – and everywhere religious icons were to be seen. During siesta time, the place was mostly empty, and then all of a sudden it was teeming with life.

We went on to visit the lovely small town of Giovinazzo with its beautiful port bathed in sunshine; there were, however, no beaches to speak of, only rocky promontories – but some of us managed to have a swim on the tiny rocky shore while our smallest child and I just sat there on the edge of the water. This charming town had the usual piazza, empty during the strongest hours of sunshine, leaving the place almost entirely to us – something we were to encounter time and time again. In the evening, we heard from our eldest son back in the UK who'd had some wonderful marks for his A Level exams; it could not have been better news and we were extremely happy and relieved. It was a shame he was not there with us to celebrate such brilliant results!

On to Alberobello, an unusual town of whitewashed cone-like houses called trulli, and which was a real picture postcard place. So pretty and appealing in fact, that it was a real delight to wander through its streets despite the more visible touristy influence, albeit a mostly Italian one. It seemed the other parts of the world did not know of this amazing place.

These trulli came into existence so as to avoid the taxman, we were told. We left this gorgeous place for a day excursion to Locorotondo, a place more reminiscent of a French town with a wonderful panorama over the countryside. On our return to Alberobello, the night welcomed us with horrible mosquitoes which kept on stinging our little one, and we could not do much apart from put some product on him and hope for the best.

We then proceeded inland (with some difficulty, using trains and hitchhiking as there was no more public transport that day) to beautiful white Ostuni with its Arabic look, perched on a mountain with brilliant whitewashed cubes on the cliff dominating the plain below. The whole place was dazzling and there was also some racing going on – a lot of activity this time! The next day, we were walking to try and reach the beach and had walked for an hour with still no sight of it; luckily, we were given a lift to this faraway beach by who else but the Mayor of Ostuni himself. This beautiful town was comprised of arch after arch of pure white with some bright pink flowers cascading down from pots. Personally, I found it hard to extricate myself from such pure beauty and the children appreciated it too, discovering street after street. For them, it was like a little adventure, and the beach had been sandy and delightful.

Lecce was next on our itinerary, but we were stuck at the station as there were very few trains in the afternoon. One had to be very careful about that in this part of Italy, and it was just as well we had brought some travelling games with us! Yet again, we had much difficulty in finding a hotel in Lecce, which did not have enough accommodation for this time of the year, and thus we ended up in a seminary. Lecce was quite different with some intricate brown architecture, quite beautiful in its own right, but we had been somewhat frustrated here and were glad to catch a nice air-conditioned bus to Otranto.

We were able to head back to the beach at Otranto where we were met with the beautiful old fortified walls, a Norman-built cathedral, and a castle, with the fortifications dominating the port – it was very beautiful!

We had a lovely kiwi drink in the evening after a quick show within the walls of the castle – quite a boring spectacle which we left pretty quickly, laughing in the warm air. While we were in this area, we visited the famous local caves called Zinzulusa, much to the children's pleasure.

Puglia possesses another Gallipolli, a lovely town surrounded by massive walls and more medieval streets in an ochre tint this time, but yet again there were some problems with accommodation.

It was a shame that Gallipolli was so noisy with motorbikes, as it was such a jewel of a place with some magnificent architecture and Roman ruins in the middle of the town, plus a beach with a deliciously warm sea below the tower and some truly massive walls. Our boy had one fall after another on this holiday, though, which was a shame, but luckily we had water and cotton wool with us practically all the time and the sea to clean the wounds, poor chap!

We finished our trip at Rome (taking the night train this time rather than the more expensive Eurostar) where we were given delightful watermelon which was so refreshing. It is funny how these little details actually make a lot of the holidays. The whole trip was a delight, although prices were surprisingly high for this area and accommodation as well as transport was a problem sometimes; however, all in all the holiday was appreciated by the adults and children alike. Southern Italy is perhaps not always cheaper than the north because Italians from the north head towards these beautifully preserved medieval towns. Who can blame them? It has so much to offer that you may as well forget about famous Tuscan, despite the prices.

Sardinia

JULY 2002

Well, how strange, good old Italy had us mesmerised again. We settled this time for a brief trip to Sardinia, the island just below Corsica. We tend to like islands as they give you sea and often mountains with history alongside; I only wish I could swim better to take full advantage of it.

Sardinia was another gorgeous place with high prices yet again. Luckily we did have some cheap flights to reach the island; I was actually scared stiff on the flight as the plane had suddenly dropped altitude and a few people uttered a scream. Thank goodness nothing was actually wrong with the plane, or at least we were not told about anything.

We arrived late as this was a charter flight, and our mistake this time was to not have booked a hotel previously for at least the first night, throwing all caution aside. Armed with a phone card and some basic Italian (yes, we could still use phone cards then, as mobiles had not been as popular as they are now) I phoned various places, and found they were full everywhere – what a start! Eventually, we found someone who had a couple of rooms in a house that were put at our disposal. The house was lost in the countryside and they had to come and pick us up, but this was quite fun as we had the house to ourselves in the middle of nowhere. The next day, they brought breakfast to us and then dropped us in the city centre for the day, collecting us again in the evening, so we had no complaint. We thought it was good of them, but also that it was part of the price as it was not cheap and there was no other way to reach the city centre, which was a few kilometres away.

Alghero was a lovely old ochre town with its harbour below its impressive walls. We stayed in Alghero for two nights, visiting some of the northern coast and when we were about to leave our hosts, we offered them a drink which they gladly accepted. But the next day, as we were about to depart, they wanted us to pay for the petrol they had used to fetch us. This was not part of the deal and a rather expensive affair – so much for great hosts!

Still, we went on and forgot about this experience and headed towards gorgeous Bosa, where we found a place belonging to a lovely couple who taught during the year and rented their second place in the summer. The room was simple but we had a delightful little yard where we gorged ourselves on grapes. Bosa was divided into two parts: the harbour/beach and the old town, half an hour's walk from the beach, where we had our breakfast.

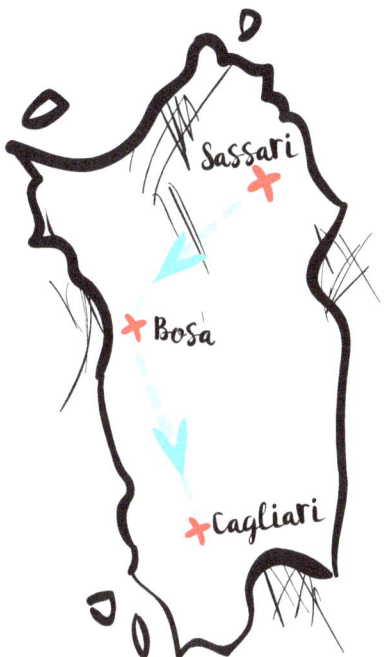

While we walked from one part to the other, we invented a song about Bosa, a beautiful town with the river zigzagging to the sea, a red roof skyline totally unspoilt – without any high-rise towers at all to my delight – along with a very peaceful atmosphere. We also sated our taste for the beach, as the weather was much nicer than we had in Alghero.

We also visited some very old remnants in the countryside, which was quite a nice distraction and had us climbing the hills again in the middle of nowhere.

Our next destination took us to Porto Rotondo, the luxury town in Sardinia where Berlusconi spends some time with his family. There were antique and fashion shops galore and yachts gleaming in the sunshine. This was more of a prefabricated town but done tastefully nevertheless, and we simply admired the lifestyle of the few.

We finished our trip around Sassari, with its beautiful rocky outcrop and the town below it, staying at a great hotel with magnificent views of this jewel. The sunsets over the Sassari buildings were quite majestuous, and it was a great place to finish a ten day trip this time. A fairly short trip as Allan and I had had previous trips to Florida on a conference and also another week in Australia (which was going to change our life upside down literally, considering it is called Down Under), but that is another story and other trips cover our time there. Here are a few of the photographs around Sassari to finish off this brief but sweet tour in Sardinia. 📍

Long Weekend in Dubai

JULY 2003

We were on our way to immigrate to Australia and as Allan was not going to have any holidays before Christmas, we thought we might as well have a break in Dubai – where I did book the hotel in advance. As this was for a short time it was something worth doing, and of course while it did not involve backpacks this time – but instead tonnes of luggage – it is still worth mentioning as this was quite different and our first real look into Arabian countries.

Dubai, back then, was a mixture of the old – with light ochre walls and latticed buildings – and the new, modern high-rises (which were going to be the main landmark from then on). We enjoyed visiting the older part and went on the river in lovely old wooden boats contrasting with the glass high-rises around its shores.

The most fascinating part of this trip was a day excursion to the actual desert which included a camel ride; a drive in a huge four-wheel drive on the dunes (quite scary); dinner under the stars in the desert; henna painting, which Vivienne and I tried (and which lasted for over three weeks, not such a pretty sight to behold later on in Australia); and belly dancing in the warm Arabian night – the whole lot.

The dunes and desert seemed to go on forever even though this was only an hour away from busy Dubai; it was quite an experience, and our first proper dunes.

Of course we must not forget the camel ride and our children being enchanted by this new experience. We had been on a camel before on the beach in Tunisia when I was pregnant with Vivienne, although I did not know it then! However, this was quite different in a real desert, and I just managed to sit on it this time while the others had a ride on these haughty but rather nice creatures.

Then it was time to get ourselves dressed in the traditional Arab garb. There was quite a flowery dress for me, nicer than the black clothes usually worn by women which hid most of their figure and face behind a chador/veil, with only the eyes showing.

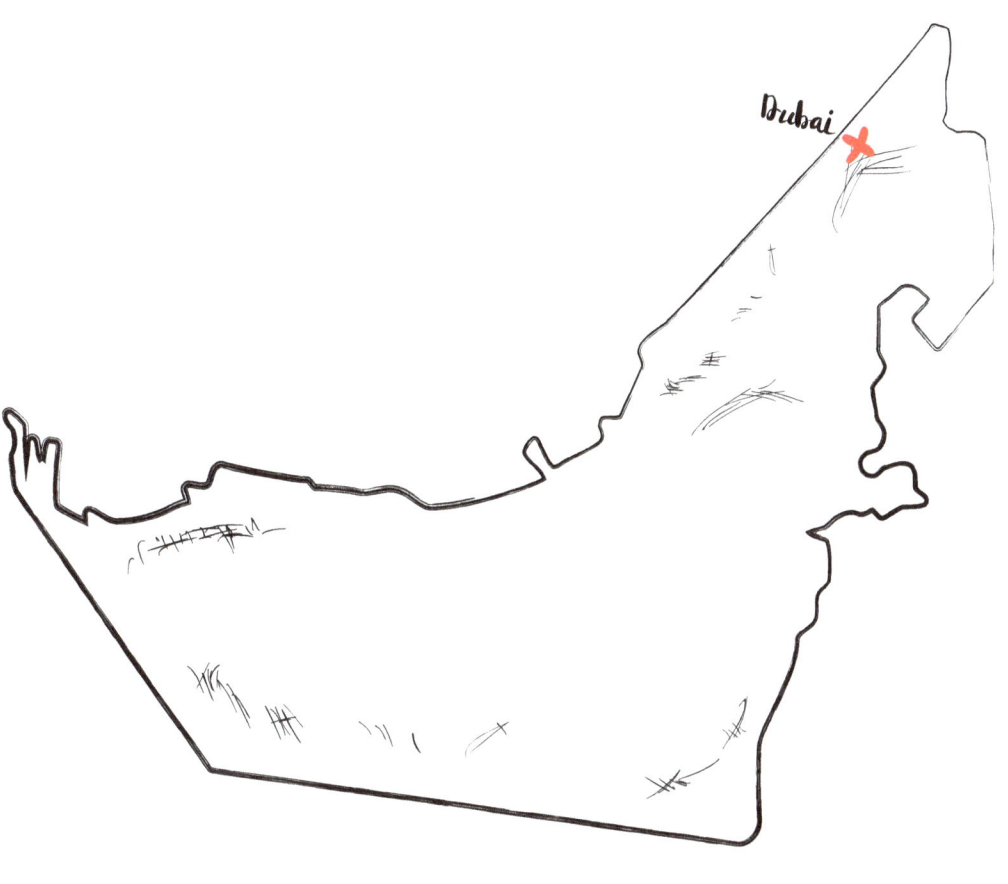

It seemed sad to me to hide behind those probably very hot clothes; our choice of clothes was definitely prettier, and we looked like Lawrence of Arabia and his wife.

We spent some time in the desert at night, to enjoy the last of this unusual day. I would have liked to go on like Scheherazade and the thousand and one nights under the magical skies of the desert. After having admired the professional belly dancer's dance, we were treated to some delicious food and belly dancing for all of us tourists. It was a good night to remember before reaching a totally different place and facing reality and work and routine on the other side of the world – a pretty daunting prospect. 📍

TRIP FROM SYDNEY TO MELBOURNE

XMAS HOLIDAYS 2003

We moved to Australia with the two smaller children, aged 15 and 9 and a half, and had a few trips whenever possible within and outside Australia because of work, and we were in need of sunshine for more than a few weeks at a time. We did not have any backpacking trips inside Australia, but I thought it would be worth just mentioning the odd trip anyway. Australia lends itself more to the car like North America, and indeed life in Australia reminds me so much of life in the States, where you do depend on the car so much – too much most likely, but that is another story.

Our first holiday after having arrived in Sydney was a week to drive down to Melbourne so as to discover a bit more of this huge island. We visited the capital, Canberra, and then went closer to the sea at Lakes Entrance with its 90-mile beach. Some of those beaches were so vast. On this holiday, we had a stopover in a little place called Sale and I ate the nicest burger I have ever had.

We experienced our very first pine trees with their branches the other way round, then crossed some scenery reminiscent of Wales with the barren hills, and a little bit of the States with the picturesque small churches in the middle of nowhere. We had one of many picnics in this land blessed by so much sunshine and such vast spaces before heading for the big city.

We arrived in the big, sprawling city that is Melbourne, with interesting architecture dotted among the skyscrapers (quite a prominent feature of Australian cities). We had some time on the beach at famous St Kilda where we encountered our first Aborigines, some woman swearing at her man for ogling other women, using quite colourful language which I would not want to repeat here. There was a mixture of quite old and new buildings, similar to Sydney and which I noted everywhere else. Vivienne and I of course had to see the place where the series *Neighbours* was filmed, which we had both been watching (looking back, I am a little ashamed) in Europe. I think I was watching it because it made me think of the sun that I was missing so much in the UK, the worst aspect of an otherwise quite beautiful place – but I digress. This place was miles away from the city centre and hard to locate, but we did eventually and upon arriving, I had quite a strange feeling.

We drove back up to a lovely, quaint and old place with traditional buildings called Albury which was and still is probably one of my favourite towns in Australia. The town was so well preserved without any odd high-rise building marring the beautiful, peaceful town. It opened my eyes to something that I have noticed time and time again after having lived in this vast country for so many years; the smaller places were the best preserved ones, and have not suffered the taint of 'progress'. The old colonial buildings were intact and showing what life would have been like over hundred or so years ago. We captured a beautiful sunset above the mighty river flowing on the edge of the town. Following this charming visit, we proceeded onwards to Holbrook, whose claim to fame was a submarine strangely and precariously resting on a raised premonitory far away from any sea. Afterwards it was onto Gundagai, with the typical New South Wales scenery; brown bare hills, with various shades of brown all over. Some of these hills were covered with beautiful white flowers or purple agapanthus, giving a joyful light to the scenery, especially when these elegant flowers rose high above the delicate white fence at the station.

This was a great introduction to such a huge place and we marvelled at the long distances and the big skies reminiscent of good old Texas, feeling perhaps a little less lost in the big wide world, far away from everyone we knew. Alas, time was of the essence and we had to return to Sydney and work.

FROM SYDNEY TO BRISBANE

Australia

EASTER 2004

Before we headed for our next holiday to discover more of this vast country, we had our eldest child's visit in Sydney. It was lovely for all of us to be together again, albeit for a short time. The photograph on the previous page captures our three kids together, quite a rarity nowadays sadly.

On our next break, we wanted to discover more of the coast north of Sydney for a change; we had ten days to do so and luckily an almost new car which could take all the mileage. We did not have a proper map at first, something I tend to forget on long trips (not the best of ideas) but found one at a petrol station. We drove to Tea Gardens off the highway and crossed a bridge over some wonderful subtropical scenery with many pelicans and herons; and we were able to have a walk over an unspoilt beach reminiscent of the Florida beaches. The next day we reached Port Macquarie with a great coastline and a splash of colourful flowers everywhere with the azure sea in the background, under a light blue sky. As it was Easter, we went to church in some pretty church on top of a hill, then watched the Easter parade in the streets. We even saw our first wild koala on a walk down some back roads, a fairly unusual sight as the koala population is suffering from disease and their environment is being destroyed by us.

Our next port of call was Coffs Harbour (Allan jokes about 'cough's harbour') a smaller but pretty town also. It has a wonderful botanical garden with subtropical plants and climate; also there was some rainforest, delightful under a perfect blue sky. While we were promenading we saw a huge lizard looking like a big slug that we have not encountered since.

One most famous attractions in this part of the world was the Big Banana theme park as there were, of course, banana plantations in Queensland; we have noticed time and again the "Big" whatever in various places in Australia. There are very few castles due to its relatively recent past of European civilisation, and nature is the big attraction in this part of the world. We visited this theme park which, a few years later, was no longer in existence, but has apparently since been revived through some organisation or other.

We drove further up to Moonie Beach, a favourite for Allan, where he was able to go for a swim into the waves. Moonie Beach is a long beach with small rivulets leading to the actual sea. We drove on to Grafton, lined with huge jacaranda trees which would have looked superb at the right season; the place was quite small and quite ghost-like in the evening.

The next day saw us celebrating our daughter Vivienne's sixteenth birthday – already sixteen! We awakened in our nice Spanish-looking hotel with white arches and flowers and drove on to Ballina. Ballina itself was somewhat disappointing as it was just houses and houses along the beach with a very busy road indeed, although we did see an iguana-type of lizard (goanna) on the rocks; further on was Lennox Head with a beautiful lookout over a wild sea, and Lake Ainsworth where the water was tainted by tea trees (an amazing natural tree which is very good for your skin and many other ailments).

We reached Byron Bay where we went to see the lighthouse, and found a good hotel in the bohemian-like town with restaurants galore.

We had a giant pizza and a 'spider' drink consisting of lemonade with some ice cream inside – not so healthy, but a very delicious way to celebrate Vivienne's birthday. We had a lovely walk on the headland, under mist and rain; this was quite a reminder of South Wales, but the bad weather did not deter us from our plan or from noticing that the place was quite beautiful and mysterious in the mist.

Tweed Heads was our next stop on the road to Brisbane. It was quite a busy place and not as interesting, but did have an Aborigine site where we walked along marshes – or rather mangroves; our first set of mangroves with many tiny orange crabs everywhere, unfortunately accompanied by unpleasant mosquitoes. We then drove to Danger Point where Captain Cook nearly shipwrecked. This was not surprising as there were huge waves crashing below us – not the place to go for a swim on a day like this, and thus we had a safe and lovely picnic overlooking the sea.

Brisbane was our last port of call before returning to Sydney. Brisbane centre had a few beautifully well preserved buildings and large pavements with some high-rise buildings in the CBD.

I did not realise then that we (husband, youngest son, and myself; we seem to be dropping kids one by one) were going to live in Brisbane where I am now writing all this; in fact, it is just my youngest son and myself by this time, as I will explain during future trips. We met up in town with Matthew, an ex-student of my husband after having had a good day's sightseeing. Before that, Allan thought of going to the University of Queensland where one of his acquaintances from Nottingham worked, and we took a taxi there as it was quite a distance from the centre itself. The building was a nice pink colonnaded one; but unfortunately this person was not there and we took the CityCat back to the centre – quite a pleasant experience.

We stopped at the botanical gardens along the river and these were very peaceful and adorned with some lovely buildings, such as the old Parliament building in the picture where we had an interesting talk about its workings. We visited the cathedral, which looked so tiny next to the high-rises around it. Like all big cities in Australia, the few old buildings remaining and likely to stay were surrounded by high-rises and the contrast was striking; I just wondered where this would all stop with the high-rises dominating the cute old buildings in a strange way.

We then had a long trip back from Brisbane, driving past Surfers Paradise which our daughter Vivienne wanted to see, so we had a short walk along and in the sea with quite huge waves; it was a rather dangerous looking sea, and we played with a nice spongy arrow that we had found previously. The place looked very packed with high-rises along the endless beach which were blocking the sunshine. In order to get out of the place, a quite frustrating drive crawling along the resorts with many traffic lights was required before joining the highway at long last.

We drove back towards Ballina where we did visit the tea plantation we had not seen on the way up. It was quite interesting, showing us the benefits of that plant and also a humorist tree with teapots on it.

We stopped at a motel in Coffs Harbour on the way back before the last leg straight to Sydney the next day for the end of this holiday – one of the last holidays with our daughter. I remember it with emotion, wishing the clock could slow down.

New Zealand

31ST DECEMBER 2004 TO 17TH JANUARY 2005

We left Sydney for our summer holiday in the afternoon, leaving our son Jim behind, and in hindsight we should have booked a flight for him to accompany us as it would have given us more time together while he was living in the same place. Unfortunately we cannot change the past and have to live with it. The trip was quite cheap as we were leaving on the last day of the year, when everyone wanted to party. The airport was indeed almost empty, and I had a thought for the poor people who had gone on holidays around this time in the tsunami-struck areas; that infamous tsunami had caused so much death and devastation in vast areas of the world.

We arrived in the evening of the New Year and walked from our hotel to get some treats such as crisps, chocolate, and drinks to celebrate the arrival of this brand new year.

However, we soon fell asleep and slept until quite late in the morning in our respective bedrooms (we had booked two for the four of us). Eventually, we headed for the centre of Christchurch, a lovely town which looked so much like a pretty English town that it had the effect of transporting us back to Europe for a short while. This was before the earthquake a few years ago destroyed this lovely and charming place, including most of this beautiful cathedral which we were lucky to see intact.

We took the bus to go and visit the Antarctic Centre, a very interesting place and so different to the typical museum. There we experienced the cold of the Antarctic in a room where very cold temperatures were artificially induced, and had to put on a coat and plastic shoes. It was quite a funny experience, but give me the desert! There was a beautiful film about the actual Antarctic which is not so far away from New Zealand, and it also showed that dressed as we were, we would not last more than thirty seconds: quite a chilling thought, excuse the pun!

In the afternoon, we went on to visit the historical quarter along the Avon River; the buildings were very pretty with willows brought back from St Helene where Napoleon died, and there was also a pretty Spanish-looking area with pastel colours.

All in all, Christchurch was a gorgeous place, not too big and not too small, and it was quite cool with grey skies reminding us of the UK in most aspects. The wooden houses were very different from the "Federation houses' of Sydney, and it was a real change of scenery.

The following day, we left lovely Christchurch and took our rented car in direction of Hanmer Springs where we were greeted by mountainous alpine scenery with little chalets all over, and sulphurous waters. We had an invigorating walk in the forest right to the top which offered a great view all around us over the surrounding mountains. The sun was back on track, so we had a lovely picnic on the edge of a turquoise river just like those in Canada. Afterwards our next destination, Kaikoura, was reached through very twisty roads. The problem was that we arrived at 9 pm; this was only a small town with many tourists as it was most famous for its maritime life such as dolphins, seals, whales, and albatross ... and all the hotels and bed and breakfast places were full. We even looked outside the town but found nothing and we were getting short of petrol, so we retraced our path to Kaikoura and eventually just found a parking place in some car park by the sea and slept in the car! The temperature was fairly cool and the car was not the most comfortable place, but we managed to grab some sleep throughout the night.

In the morning, we woke up to find many other cars there when there had been hardly any the previous night; this was the place where you could go on a boat to look for whales – what a stroke of luck! Therefore, dressed in many layers of clothes as it was back to clouds and a grey sky, we went to the reception area and were lucky enough to find that there was still room for us to go on the boat. Had we been later, we would not have been so lucky, but being on the spot helped. The cost was definitely not cheap but since we had not paid any accommodation the previous night, it made up for it. We were lucky to be able to see three huge humpback whales, and even the sun came back to greet us.

The weather was still quite brisk; that December had been the coldest in sixty years apparently. We had a picnic by the sea, talking to some Irish/British couple, and drove a little bit further to where we were able to see some seals – such amazing creatures. Some Korean children were throwing stones at them, so Allan quickly told them off and they stopped their cruel game. We had to leave this dreamlike place for our next place, Picton, where yet again we had some difficulties finding accommodation, but eventually managed to find a superb bed and breakfast with magnificent views over the Marlborough Sounds. These views were fjord-like, and simply some of the most beautiful views I have ever seen from a house! Biscuits, fruit, tea, and coffee were at our disposal as well as a superb breakfast the next day.

We went for a walk in the little town; decidedly New Zealand has some of the most incredible scenery in the world, on a smaller scale than Canada although similar to some extent, but it is just so beautiful! This was the view we woke up to!

Then we left our splendid place and the rain came and made it all look too similar to Wales, and we arrived in Nelson where we found another bed and breakfast. Bed and breakfasts are great places to stay as it means that not only do you usually have a superb breakfast but also that you meet other people, or at least the owners of the place.

Our gorgeous breakfast made up for the weather and spirits went back up. We did not meet people in this B&B, but there was an absolute trust as they just expected us to leave the money before leaving. Then we left for St Arnaud and a lake with forests all around, and had a muddy walk as the paths were soaked in places due to the rain the day before.

Vivienne lost her shoe in the mud and her whole foot sunk in, to her displeasure. We arrived at the car just before the rain came back with a vengeance and reached Reefton, a picturesque little town where we went to have a hamburger while the rain was still falling.

We went for a walk in the morning before leaving the town of Reefton, which was the first town to have electricity in Australasia, and went to visit an old shack in the town where an old bearded man showed us how people used to live at the beginning of the twentieth century; we did some gold prospecting before going on the road again. This was very interesting, along with a quick visit of the museum attached to the shack.

We went as far as Hotikita with a pale sun deigning to show itself, and there we found another B&B. We had a walk along the grey beach covered with boughs which gave some great time to the 'blokes' among us as they visited some sort of Maori tent. Later on we had some soup, pizza, and strawberries with our hosts. Before going to bed, we went to see the glow worms which shone in the night in order to attract flies and devour them, quite an interesting and unusual show with hundreds of tiny lights.

The next morning was Allan's birthday and we were greeted by a great breakfast of toast, cereals, eggs, fruit, tea, and coffee with our pleasant hosts. He had been a gold prospector and showed us some gold; apparently a Japanese lady thought he was showing something to eat and tried to eat some of his gold!

Then, after having visited his shop – (which was alongside the B&B) where we bought one of their knives – we were on the road again to take the glaciers road.

We were accompanied by rain and sun intermittently, and saw the Franz Joseph Glacier. We were hoping to find accommodation at the place itself but it was all very expensive, and this time found a basic backpacker, and were then able to walk on the moraine, little pebbles and paths above some brooks. We could not reach the summit of this glacier as it was too dangerous to climb up without a guide, but it was still very pleasant. The next day saw us climbing the Fox Glacier and that was quite arduous with a tunnel of ice at the end; we were lucky that the weather remained clement during the whole climb there and back, and the rain started just when we reached the car. We met some lady who could only go half way up the glacier because the tour she was part of only allowed around forty-five minutes to go up and back, which was definitely not enough. This served again to represent how much better it was to fly on our own wings most of the time and spend the time as we liked, without rushing. The moraine had a turquoise tint that was making me think of some huge ice cream.

We then tried to reach Matheson Lake in the hope of seeing Mt Cook, but the dense cloud formation was preventing us from actually seeing the mount, so we just walked briefly before leaving for Haast on the coast and bought a postcard of the most famous mount. Then we reached the picturesque town of Wanaka where the children went to a labyrinth at Puzzling World and had great fun while we just waited for them with some tea/coffee whilst talking to a Scottish man who had been dealing with horse races in South Africa.

The next port of call was quite far, so we were on our way after a brief picnic near the lake in Wanaka for our next destination, the beautiful town of Queenstown, most famous for winter sports.

We left quite early the next morning to do the route of *The Lord of the Rings* which had been filmed in this location and that the kids definitely wanted to see. The scenery was even more impressive and the sun was bright for once, rendering the colour of the lake even more beautiful and striking, and the mountains so much clearer against the blue sky. We were extremely lucky to see this beauty under sunshine; New Zealand has to be one of the most beautiful places in the world as far as scenery goes.

Here are a couple of pictures to prove the almost indescribable beauty; it was almost unreal and perfect. Upon arrival in Glenorchy, we asked to go horse riding; this proved to be too expensive, but Allan and the children were able to do so later on somewhere else. So we went back to Queenstown for a picnic along the lake and booked a hotel in Lumsden.

From there, we were able to go to Deer Park Heights on the mountain above the lake, with staggering views so typical of *The Lord of the Rings*. Vivienne recognized some places in the film and was delighted. There, we were able to feed some small horses, goats, and sheep around us – a lovely experience.

From Lumsden, we had a short drive to Te Anau, a cute little town with a large avenue, pretty shop windows, and a lake at the end of the town. New Zealand definitely has a large number of lakes and that increases its beauty. Water, whether in the shape of lakes, rivers, or the sea always adds beauty to a place. After having booked our hotel and a horse riding trip for Allan and the children, we drove to picturesque Milford Sound. This was quite a drive, but a beautiful one with snow not far away and the graceful meadow covered with all sorts of pretty, soft wild flowers facing the majestic rocky figure of the mountains all around. There is only one word for this: splendid! We had a quick picnic and were just in time to catch the boat, which was going to take us and other tourists gently gliding through the fjord despite the strong wind. We passed a waterfall and a colony of seals lounging on the rocks, ignorant of us. The boat went as far as the mouth of the sea before returning, and from there it was back to Te Anau. We learnt later on in the evening of Allan's uncle Peter's passing in Italy, and Allan and I had a quick walk and a drink in a pub on our own in the evening talking about him.

After an early start and leaving our lovely room, we drove to the place where my family – excluding me due to my hip problems – was going to start their horse riding six kilometres away. Perched on these elegant horses, they looked so high off the ground. Marc actually galloped, which they were not supposed to do, but they had a good time for a couple of hours while I went back to Te Anau and bought myself a T-shirt, did some shopping for lunch time, and sunbaked – as the Australians would say – on the grass facing the lake, looking at kayaks.

Then it was time to leave this enchanting town to take a long drive from west to east, stopping en route to do some sightseeing and stretch our legs at Gore and Clinton (the presidential road of Gore and Clinton), to arrive in Dunedin where we found a motel without any problem; it did not look like much from the outside, but was superb and ultra-modern inside with a pretty combination of beige and dark brown shades. We visited the pretty university and Baldwin Street, the steepest street in the world apparently, and we were out of breath when we reached its top – well at least I was. The town and its streets were very reminiscent of a Welsh town, with some lovely grey stone buildings, many churches and cathedrals, and lovely villas; all in all quite a prosperous Victorian town, and very impressive.

In the morning, we visited the one and only castle that exists in New Zealand, Larnac Castle, a well restored mansion according to Vivienne with beautiful gardens just like in the UK and even a similar temperature; its walls were made from materials from all over the world. We had coffee/tea and biscuits in the ballroom – quite civilised! Despite the natural beauty of the place, this historical castle was a nice diversion, something that I miss around this part of the world really. The views of little islands and a lake were superb.

Then it was on to Oamaru going past huge boulders on the beach; these boulders were almost perfect and so round. This town was also historic and full of lovely white limestone buildings, another smaller version of Leamington Spa, the Victorian town I had fallen in love with (where we lived close by before moving to Australia with its shimmering white buildings dating from the Victorian area). After the fairly quick visit to this graceful town, we went to look for the yellow-eyed penguins; rare penguins which inhabit this area and that we were lucky enough to see on the beach, aided by some binoculars.

Sadly, after this we returned to Christchurch, which meant the holiday was soon coming to an end. We went back to the same hotel we had stayed in when we arrived, but were in a nicer bedroom which even had a Jacuzzi. We meant to go and visit Timaru where there was supposed to be a park and a large aviary, but somehow we could not find it, so we went to the pretty village of Geraldine instead. Geraldine hosted one of our many picnics and the weather had turned for the best; it was actually quite hot and the sun was very bright. On the way back to Christchurch, we were arrested by the police as it seems we were exceeding the speed limit, but got away with just a reprimand.

We spent the next day in the very pretty French town of Akaroa; to reach it you drive down a steep pass towering above the little town. This valley, cut from volcanoes, lies next to a sea so blue with mountains on either side. The town itself is covered with French names in all the streets as the French had emigrated there in the past. So, of course, I wanted to ask for a baguette in a baker's shop and the shop assistant asked me with some surprise: "A bag of what?" Hmm, obviously her ancestors were not French. Anyway this gave us much laughter later on and a good joke to tell my French students. This was actually pretty incredible as most people know the word 'baguette' in most places in the world. Allan and Marc went kayaking while Vivienne and I returned to the car so she could change to something cooler, and then we both went on a *pedalo* and had a lovely time. Allan and I even went for a swim later on in a fairly cold sea, I must admit. Summer had at long last arrived, a bit late as we were soon to leave New Zealand, but we were still lucky enough to experience it.

The next day was our last full day on this wonderful island and we had to give our car back. Afterwards, we wandered in the botanical garden to relax in front of the fountain, and then visited a market where they were exhibiting crafts. There was also some Irish dancing in a beautiful building belonging to the university where we were able to enjoy some lovely French pancakes or Hungarian pancakes – whichever they were, they were delicious. Then, we went back to the botanical garden full of roses and a greenhouse and lovely lawns looking more like the European lawns we used to know. That reminded me of my grandmother who used to say that grass was the same everywhere; well, I can vouch that it is not. Lastly, we had a brief visit in a museum which was really interesting but that we had to leave early, as we were running out of time. Early the next day we had to get back to Sydney and a cool 18 degree temperature; three and a half hours away by plane, where our eldest child awaited us.

In summary, New Zealand was a glorious holiday with so many various activities in such beautiful scenery – mountains, lakes, and rivers – that I would definitely recommend visiting to anyone. The weather can be capricious, that is true, but its beauties defy even the worst weather. It was not a cheap holiday, but worth every penny! You only go round once as someone said to us back in good old Texas when we bought our car, and this statement – which is so true – was never forgotten by Allan or me.

Broken Hill and the Outback

LONG WEEKEND ANZAC 23RD TO 26TH APRIL 2005

As we wanted to see as much as possible of Australia and other countries, whenever there was more than a weekend available we shot off somewhere; this time, with just Marc in tow, we decided to get a feel of the Outback. The closest possible reliable "Outback experience" was around Broken Hill, a town that I had noticed on the map on the plane and somehow was keen to see. The easiest way was to actually take the train and then the bus for the long journey, around ten hours altogether, so we had to get up at dawn, around 5.30 am, to catch a bus for the station and the train. We knew at that time that the Australian adventure was coming to a close – or so we thought – so we had to see what the red earth of the Outback looked like. The trip there was actually pretty cheap to our surprise, and if all the other trains were as cheap, it would be great.

The train went through Bathurst, Orange where we'd had a long weekend some time earlier, and finally stopped at Dubbo after six or seven hours' journey. This was the first time we saw many Aborigines, and we took a full bus to go for the last leg of the journey. The countryside suddenly changed, and the trees became rarer as the earth got redder. We stopped in Cobar to get ourselves some food; a family of Aborigines ate some greasy fish and chips and, of course, the kids got sick on the bus soon afterwards.

Marc spotted some kangaroos from the bus and I spotted three emus. On the train, we spoke to some people who had lived in Broken Hill and were returning there; one of them had been the nurse for the famous painter Pro Hart while the other was a young Danish musician who was going to teach for three months at a cattle station, north of Broken Hill. The bus was moving fast and the night was coming; the trees were almost non-existent by now and were replaced by bushes here and there, and some desert. I could see kangaroos and, of course, these poor creatures were jumping right in front of the bus, attracted by the lights, and we could hear the impact of these poor animals being hit, many of them being more active at night.

We arrived in Broken Hill around 11 pm, quite tired by then, but this was different from jet lag.

We met up again with the older couple we had met on the train whose hotel was just opposite ours, and we made plans to meet them again during this long weekend; they lived in Wentworth Falls in the Blue Mountains. Our room was simple but quite big, with two single beds and a double bed – Vivienne could have come with us. We slept fairly well apart from being disturbed in the middle of the night by people arguing outside.

The next day we went first thing to the tourist office for various tidbits of information and then rented a car, a great white Toyota. We then set out for the ghost town of Silverton, a town that was famous for advertising Coca-Cola and beer, and for the various films that had been shot in its environs; the Mad Max prop car sat in front of a café.

The earth was indeed red and arid and very dusty, but the small town in this isolated corner was quite charming; we visited the old prison, and felt so far away from Sydney – like a whole world away. Then we went to Mundi Mundi where we could see the shape of the planet with superb 360 degree views right up to the dam, which had become just a big puddle of water, such was the dryness of the area.

We went as far as Menindee, quite a banal town with not much going for it apart from the fact that the road that goes there shows the whole expanse of desert going on and on for miles, flat and desolate. Menindee was most famous for the hotel where Will & Burke, explorers, stayed before setting out on their famous expedition in 1860-61; it was the last place they were seen before disappearing forever.

On the way back to Broken Hill, we noticed an actual lake where children were swimming, and then took the long road back to BH with the sun getting lower in the horizon. Despite quite a lovely sunset over this desolate part of Australia, we were getting more and more worried about kangaroos, visible now on the side of the road. Luckily we arrived without any problem, and were quite relieved.

Our last day in Broken Hill – Anzac Day – was spent around the town itself, going to see the beautiful Living Desert sculptures on the hill. The twelve sandstone artworks majestically stand over the town, originally sculpted from the stone by sculptors from all over the world. They were quite a magnificent, unique sight to behold.

After touring this unforgettable site, we regretfully went back to the arty town and watched some of the Anzac Day celebrations – not my favourite, as these mostly have to do with the army.

Next, we visited some old silver mines and walked back to the town centre; the heat was pretty intense, we did not have the car anymore, and we were lucky to meet our acquaintances from the Blue Mountains who gave us a lift and with whom we shared a lovely ice cream – apparently some people drive for miles to have these. The buildings in the town were very nice and quite old for the country, and the next day saw us retracing our steps back to Sydney, with our heads full of lovely memories of a totally different area. I for one would love to see more of the Outback – such desolation in itself was an eye opener, and has a strange beauty.

Cairns and the Atherton Tablelands

17th TO 25th MAY 2005

We left again for one week's holiday without Vivienne, who did not want to come with us, unfortunately. We quickly said our goodbyes and left the unit very early to catch a taxi to the airport and a three hour flight with Jetstar seated in lovely grey leather seats. We had our breakfast of biscuits and rock scones, some juice and coffee, and read some of the plane's brochures; it seemed to me one of the quickest three hour flights I'd ever had.

As soon as we arrived, we noticed that Cairns was surrounded by mountains, and we were hit by the wonderful, pleasantly warm tropical heat. We took a shuttle to the city and booked a hotel room (through a tourist agency), which was nice but a little bit far from the city centre, but someone from the hotel picked us up in their van, so that was good. After a quick shower to freshen up, we had our first walk in the town to the Flecker Botanical Garden with its luxuriant vegetation; those tropical flowers were, at that time, very unusual for us to encounter and very pretty. There were all sorts of strange roots and vegetation reminiscent of Florida, with its similar weather patterns. We had a walk on a boardwalk right next to the water's edge and saw a sign warning: 'Crocodiles have been seen, don't go near the edge'. This gave us a strange feeling, imagining seeing those monsters come out of the water at any time.

We shared a taxi with some girls to go back to the Esplanade, where we strolled along the little artificial beach, gazing at the sea far away at low tide. We strolled further on to the artistic, touristy shops and booked a reef snorkelling session for the day after next at the tourist office, and worked out some details for our trip to Kuranda the next day. We were not going to take the scenic railway, as this was rather expensive, but instead took a really cheap bus – the cheapest bus I have ever been on in Australia. We were starving by then and had a delicious pizza close to a lovely square, listening to some singers who had great voices and sung the lovely tune *Sweet Home Alabama* (that I had first heard in the film of the same name, which I saw with Vivienne back in the UK near Birmingham) and then walked back to our hotel: a nice full day without being too rushed.

After a hearty breakfast of toast, cereals and juice, tea, and coffee, we left to take our mini-bus to Kuranda; as I said earlier the trip was so cheap, only two dollars each for half an hour's drive! The bus took us up to the mountains, and we had to be back at the bus stop by 3 pm, so we had no time to lose. We headed first to the Venom Zoo where the owner taught us about spiders; tarantulas; scorpions, and centipedes which could actually kill, a fact unbeknownst to us and I believe most people. It was scary, but was also a quite fascinating place. We then went to Butterfly World where there were beautiful multicoloured butterflies, and the famous Blue Ulysses. Then it was off to the market where we treated ourselves to a glorious, lovely three-fruit type of ice cream before getting back to visiting more attractions – this time Bird World. We were in among those gorgeous creatures and they were so close to us; a green parrot went and rested on Allan's shoulder briefly but I missed the photo opportunity, and then another one landed on my hand. It was really quite magical; birds have always been interesting to me ever since my childhood. In my childhood we had doves and pigeons in a big aviary where I used to go to tame them and think among my feathered friends. After we finished our session in this animal kingdom, we walked briefly through the rainforest before returning to Cairns by bus and heading once again to the artificial beach, where we had a rest on the neighbouring lawn. We then took a walk to the pretty esplanade and another walk through the night markets, where we had a small dinner before reaching our hotel. It was another full and lovely day in great temperatures.

The next day, we had to get up at 6 o'clock in order to catch the boat to take us to the reef as it was leaving just before eight. There were around twenty-eight people on board when we left Cairns; the weather lifted and the sun appeared with some small light clouds clustered around the sky, and it already felt quite warm even in T-shirts and shorts. We had tea and coffee first of all, and then were each given a mask and tube for snorkelling and sat on the top part of this fairly small boat just relaxing. After about two and a half hours, we reached Michaelmas Cay, a small outer reef island to which a dinghy took us.

The island was, just a tiny dot in the ocean without any accommodation, full of nesting birds, with a spotless sandy beach where we could walk in order to start our snorkelling.

I was becoming quite nervous; we were wearing wetsuits – and a life jacket for Marc and me – plus some flippers which made walking rather difficult, so of course I fell in the water on the soft white sand. "That is the way to do it," said someone who was working with the boat. Marc and I were beginners with the mask and snorkel, and soon water was coming in our mouths.

Allan re-adjusted our life jackets and that seemed to help, and we dared to go out of our depth into the water over the reef and fish. I just took the tube off when the water continued to creep in and breathed out of the water, then put it back to watch the wonders below, then swam back to the beach and then back out again (rinse and repeat). Allan and Marc swam back to the main boat, and this was rather brave of Marc; it was good he'd had those swimming lessons. However, he did get bitten by a fish (a trevally) which left its mark on his thigh; the fish thought he was food alongside the crumbs that people were throwing from the boat.

The boat went on to another reef, Hastings's Reef, and on the way there, we had a nice meal of cold meats, curry and rice, nice pasta, salad, and some pineapple and melon before eventually reaching the reef. (Picture at Bird World.) Here there was snorkelling from the boat and the water was much deeper and this time, so Marc and I did not go. Allan tried diving but decided against it after some scary minutes in the water and snorkelled instead while we went on a glass-bottom boat twice. Marc and I had a good time and saw quite a few fish: parrot king, clownfish, spotted sweet lip, a nice blue reef, big clams which had closed down – all great and unique sights to admire. Afterwards we returned to the main boat for some cakes and tea – quite a posh affair! The sea started being fairly rough on the way back as we talked to some English people travelling round for two to three months; their daughter had done pharmacy at Nottingham University and they knew the little village of Hatton where we lived near Birmingham, and even the little town of Flers where I come from! We also talked to a couple of Israelis who were spending nearly two years in Adelaide and travelling a lot. We were back on dry land at 5.30 pm, quite tired and sunburnt, but so happy with our trip. We then booked a hire car for the next few days before returning to our hotel for some quickly made pasta and a good night's sleep after our adventures of the day, nearly leaving Allan in the water....

After a good breakfast, we left to collect our hire car, and had problems with the agency, who were asking for more money than we thought it would cost. We went to another agency but their cost was even more expensive so, not having the luxury of choice, we returned to the first place and were lucky enough to be able to have the car at the price we originally booked. We were on our way at long last, driving along the gorgeous coast with mountains as backdrop. We stopped at Palm Cove, a lovely beach fringed with my beloved palm trees, and relaxed there for over an hour, playing with Marc and throwing our cute little plastic arrow (which we thought we had lost), then had a stroll along the beach. In the pictures below, which one is the biggest or the most elegant? No need to reply, it's the bird!

We travelled on, had a small rest, and then drove to Hartley's Crocodile Farm, arriving early afternoon. That whole afternoon was a show of crocodiles on the farm – loads of them on top of each other – then the usual snake show, but the young man was very entertaining. He knew a lot and everything was delivered with enthusiasm and a good sense of humour. Then two men entered the crocodile's arena, tempting it with food. I don't think he was that hungry but it was still very fascinating to see its jaws opening and closing with a loud bang. All this was followed by a half hour cruise on the green lagoon with the guide teasing the crocs in the water who opened their menacing jaws against the boat, jumping from the water. The time soon went, and we ended the afternoon with a brief tour to look at the other crocs and the gentler koalas, which we stroked.

The place felt a bit sad though, considering that most of these crocs would end up as food or leather for bags and belts, although this crocodile farm did mean that there were no crooks hunting them in the wild where they would be unprotected. You have to balance one against the other.

We then headed for Port Douglas where we found a cheap motel with a white and red scheme, with white wicker furniture and an oldish bathroom which was perfectly adequate for our needs. Marc did not feel too well that evening, perhaps because we had not eaten for a long time, so we put him to bed for a rest and went for a quick drink, just the two of us, but returned quickly to him. It had started raining – actually, it had threatened to rain all day but there had only been a few tentative drops – and it rained pretty heavily in the night; we just hoped it would dry up for the next day's tourism.

A hearty breakfast which got thumbs up from Allan and son at a café nearby, coupled with the weather improving gradually (still on the brisk side), started the day. En route to Daintree and Cape Tribulation, we first had a stop at Mosman Gorge, which was a bit disappointing as I had heard so much about it. Then we drove to the tiny village of Daintree where we had a drink opposite the sea. Daintree was the port for boats looking for crocs. Past Daintree, we crossed some wonderful scenery of mountainous backdrops with sugar cane in front of them and proceeded to take winding roads through the rainforest, which took us past a lookout from where we could see beautiful beaches. We finally arrived at the famous Cape Tribulation, where the rainforest drops into the sea. It was quite windy and we walked along the beach, where had a chat with some American lost in this part of the world. Interesting the meetings you can have all over the world with unusual, adventurous people ready to make a living on the other side of the world far from their families and usual comforts.

We then went to another more sheltered beach where Marc indulged in sand castle building, which he enjoyed for many years; it was a joy to behold his interest in this innocent pursuit in a world too often marred by kids growing up much too quickly and losing their childhoods, willingly or unwillingly.

Next door was an interesting crocodile sand feature, and the trees along the beach bore many coconuts. It made a change from the European beaches and vegetation – so much more exotic! What we missed in historical buildings in this part of the world was exchanged for some lovely, pure, and still fairly wild scenery.

Before leaving the area, we walked near the picturesque harbour and an alluring beach which was strangely empty in the glorious weather, with just a few light cotton-like clouds floating in the sky; not the bright blue sky of Sydney, but nevertheless a lovely light with some warm mist hanging over the mountains.

As we approached this tiny beach, we noticed a sign telling us to beware the crocodiles that were present in this area – no wonder the beach was empty! In hindsight, I was a little bit silly to pose next to it, although I guessed the croc was not in the area at that time; however, we did not linger on these inviting sands.

We reluctantly left the beach and its warmish sea in the early afternoon to drive inland and reach the Atherton Tablelands; perhaps not a bad idea as we had been slightly sunburnt. There were sugar cane trains en route to Mareeba, and the rainforest was now a long way away but in its place was a drier landscape of gums – some burnt – and loads of anthills, giving the area a lunar landscape. This was the beauty of Australia; there is actually quite a large variety of scenery even within short distances. Atherton itself was full of pubs, and lacked the sophisticated appeal of Port Douglas.

We visited the lovely gardens of Chinatown; the Chinese had been responsible for developing sugar cane in the area, and it was quite odd but interesting to see an old temple here and read a story about these Chinese, who eventually had to leave. Then we drove to a crater, a huge hole with green tepid water at the bottom back in the rainforest, and then on to Millau Millau Waterfall, a very pleasant spot where we met by chance again the Israeli people we had met on the boat to the reef and we followed them to another waterfall with a very beautiful setting indeed. The world is big and small at the same time.

We had a lovely break including hot chocolate and coffee with a banana split for Marc, overlooking the romantic hilly scenery with flowers spurting everywhere. We exchanged email addresses (lost unfortunately) and parted company, heading toward the lovely old village of Yungaburra where we found accommodation for the night and had a lovely meal that we were able to bring back to the kitchen of our B&B. The owner's wife was from Leicestershire in the UK; what a contrast it must have been for her living there, far from everywhere. The husband had been bitten by a snake once and had to go to hospital and was extremely lucky to survive. We visited the huge and very impressive Yungaburra market where I bought myself a lovely white Thai top and then it was back to Cairns for the plane back to Sydney and Vivienne, who had missed out on this great unforgettable trip.

Sydney to Adelaide

13TH TO 22ND APRIL 2006

By this time, Allan was already back in the UK working and Vivienne had joined him after having finished school and leaving Australia which, in the end, she had not taken to. Marc and I stayed on in Sydney for an extra year punctuated with two months back in the UK to visit them, and it was hard for just the two of us to come back. We did this so as to give Marc the opportunity to start school in a selective school called Fort Street, where he had been admitted purely on his academic merits, so we made the sacrifice. Luckily, Allan had flexible holidays and was able to come back every six weeks to his beloved Australia. We took advantage of his trips back to do some sightseeing whenever possible, and decided on a trip to Adelaide.

So here we were on our way, on the first step of our long journey one of the first towns we crossed was Bathurst. This town is surrounded by the huge Hay plain, a yellow, sunburnt, flat land stretching for miles over the horizon. We saw the famous Murray River, so important in Australia, the most arid continent on the planet. We stopped at Mildura for a walk in a quite ordinary town and later bought a sack of oranges near Berri past 'The Big Orange', obviously very famous for its oranges and so colourful that we took a picture. In Australia, we noticed many times the 'Big' this and the 'Big' that, possibly because there is not much else outside its gorgeous scenery. We saw a 61-year-old talking cockatoo in its cage; what a lovely bird, and what a long life they can have! On the way to Adelaide, the police stopped Allan for speeding, and luckily we just had a caution, but we kept our eyes on the speedometer. We reached Adelaide on the 15th, quite a quick drive considering the huge distance covered, and we both took turns driving. At some point, while Allan was asleep and resting by Marc in the back of the car, I faced a sandstorm while driving and I had to concentrate really hard on the road. This was an experience I had never had before, but we got through it. The sky had turned yellow and there was no one else on the road, and soon we could see the Barossa in the distance – at long last a break from the flat emptiness.

I was very impressed by the town of Adelaide, much smaller than Sydney, but big enough to have all the entertainment you wanted – with its lovely historical mile: the Parliament building, the Memorial building, the Festival Centre, the University, the Convention Centre, and so on, all right in the city centre by the Torrens River.

At long last, a skyline which was hardly marred by more modern buildings; there had been some planning in this place unlike the other higgledy piggledy towns which bore a typical mishmash of old and new at random, and here the sky was not swallowed by high-rises. This town had style, and is probably my favourite among the five major cities around Australia. It had those grand old buildings and large avenues with trees reminiscent of Europe, and looked quite sophisticated and gentler to the senses. I still do not know Hobart in Tasmania to this day, so I cannot comment on that city, which I think I would like to see very much. This historical mile comprised some red brick buildings like in the UK; some stylish modern buildings in the background; the grey tiled University of Adelaide (its beautiful façade was the entrance of the botanical garden); and so many churches.

Adelaide is a town of churches, the only town which was not built by convicts, where everything was only twenty minutes' drive from the city centre – whether it was the famous villages in the hills or Glenelg by the Sea. Glenelg could be reached by tramway, and had a lovely pedestrian shopping high street; not those big indoor shopping malls which I find so barren, lacking street activity, boutiques and, above all, air...

We then headed for the Adelaide hills, seeing some lovely old cars en route, and we had a gorgeous panoramic view over the city of Adelaide below from Lofty Summit. We visited some more botanical gardens blooming in riots of colour; it was a lot cooler than the north of the country and thus had more European-like colours with the more marked seasons. The houses here were mostly made of sandstone and very pretty and solid-looking. This type of house was present first in the fairly quaint little town of Stirling, and then in the German town of Hahndorf, with the sky very blue and the light quite beautiful in these very graceful and peaceful towns.

We left this lovely area as we wanted to do the Great Ocean Road on our way back up – one of the most scenic roads in the world alongside the Pacific Coast Highway in California I believe. We were not disappointed, although the weather had worsened. We had a miserable day weather-wise, and stopped at Meningie by a lake where we had those famous sausage sizzles. Then we reached Kingston with its huge lobster where there was more rain. Luckily, by the time we reached Mount Gambier, although the temperature had taken a turn for the colder, the sun re-appeared and we were able to see the Blue Lake actually looking blue. Then it was onwards to Bridgewater on Cape Discovery Bay with its beautiful semi-circular bay that we could see in all its glory. We discovered another unusual aspect of this quite fabulous bay: the Petrified Forest near the cape.

It was all brown like the sand around it, and I had a matching jacket that made me blend in with this unusual scenery. I had never seen a petrified forest before. Nature in Australia brings you some surprises, and probably is the best aspect of this country.

We managed a walk on a beach not far from Cape Bridge when the sun came out at last, and it was lovely to walk freely and breathe the sea air; the sea itself was a pretty turquoise. Then we reached Port Fairy, a pretty little place on Great Ocean Road which was indeed quite fairy-like, with boats floating happily on the river and cottages which belonged to the whalers in the past. We stayed in one of those lovely cottages with a little kitchen, lounge, and a porch; the owner had his bigger place just behind. It was just lovely, quaint, and a good price too.

The following day, we continued on the magnificent road, starting with the Bay of islands, the great Blowhole of the Grotto, London Bridge, Lord Arch Gorge, and the Shipwreck Coast (and you could see why it was called this, with the demented sea below the majestic cliffs) with the mist and rain returning. The whole place was very impressive and the rough weather and rough seas actually added to the experience, although it did spoil our warmth and sunshine.

Lamentably, soon we had to leave this enchanting road, perhaps not giving it enough time, but we had to get back, and so went back to Geelong, close to Melbourne. Geelong was quite famous for its bollards all along the coast, and was quite an interesting and relatively big town in the area.

The weather had improved by then and the sky was a bright blue, making the bollards stand out – a jolly sight to behold.

Our last visit before heading back to beautiful Albury – and then back to Sydney – was to the very interesting Sovereign Hill in Ballarat, where people used to look for gold, and we panned like in the past. The whole place was preserved as it was in the past with people dressed up in clothes of the time adding to the authentic atmosphere.

We spent the whole day there, and it reminded me of Plymouth near Boston. There were some British guards in their old red uniforms; the gentry wearing top hats; horse-drawn carriages; wooden houses with few luxuries as they would have had in the past; roads which were muddy – quite a living museum. The temperature had grown quite cold by then, as cold as on an autumn day in the UK.

We had a good time and left for one of my favourite cities in Australia, well preserved Albury, which I was able to see a second time. This was a nice, long break which we might not have been able to enjoy as much had Allan still been working in Sydney as, while he worked in the UK, he had quite a few holidays when he could spend time with us and see some of the places without too much rush.

It was great to reconnect and be together again, the three of us, as it has been for quite a while since. Often it has seemed as if Marc had been our only child as he shared a lot of our times together, and hopefully he will cherish these times in the future. ♥

Bangkok and Ayutthaya

LONG WEEKEND: BEGINNING AUGUST 2006

Marc and I were returning, (normally definitely, but that was not going to be) to the UK to live with Allan, back in our Claygate where I had my first home with Allan and which I probably will always cherish for this reason. As we were returning via Bangkok, I thought we might as well have a long weekend there and discover more of this part of the world before returning to the west.

I had booked a hotel for two or three nights, quite luxurious and still pretty cheap. We first visited the site of the temples, which were so different from any other temples we had seen; very ornate, gold gilded, pointy columns with intricate designs, and huge statues again with so many symbols on them. The whole place was quite magical and we had a great time visiting the whole complex – wherever you looked there was something magnificent and grandiose.

After this enchanting visit, we took a tuk-tuk to visit Jim Thompson's house, which I knew was very beautiful and built with typical wood from the area. Jim Thompson had been an American who was selling silk and disappeared in the Cameron Highlands in Malaysia; nobody ever found out his whereabouts, but his house and the great silk were still there as a testimony to his time there. The house was indeed very beautiful both outdoors and indoors, and I bought a little blue silk as a reminder.

In the evening, at the hotel, I booked some Thai dances and a special meal while we were watching the dances. The cost was not exorbitant, and I thought we might as well savour some of the local culture. The choice of food was quite impressive and served in some lovely white and blue porcelain dishes, and the dances looked very elegant. The dancers were wearing elaborate costumes and their small hands were used with elegance and grace, even the male dancers accompanying the lovely and delicately-boned Thai ladies as can be seen in the picture below. It was a very entertaining evening for both of us so far away from everyone else we knew, my little son and companion and myself.

The next day saw us booking a taxi for the day to drive all the way to the ancient capital of Ayutthaya, an hour away. The taxi was incredibly cheap considering we were having it all day and stopping at various palace complexes between Bangkok and the old capital; the driver stayed in his taxi while we were visiting.

We had tried taking the train, but the hours were no good and also it would not take us to the temple complex, so we thought might as well take advantage of such a cheap offer. We first stopped to see the palace complex and walk around its grounds; these were pretty impressive and well kept, and it was a delightful walk in peaceful surroundings.

Ayutthaya itself was very impressive again with those interesting spires, but also with the old red stones and dozens of Buddha statues with orange shawls of some sort jealously guarding the temples. There were organised walks on the back of elephants, so we took advantage of this opportunity to climb on one. It was very clever the way it was organised; we just walked up some steps to a platform from where we could easily sit on some comfortable chairs on the back of the elephant for half an hour. Our elephant was walking around this glorious temple and at times it looked a bit dangerous, but it did not lose its footing under the skilful elephant master. We later sat on the trunks of two elephants; I was not too reassured I must say, but Marc seemed fine even when he was raised in the air by one; I guess he was a little anxious, but seemed pleased and it was a good photograph of something quite unusual. Luckily, those elephants are rather smaller than the African ones and seemed to have a good and placid temperament.

Back at the entrance, we were sitting at a café to have some refreshment and noticed two small tigers playing together and a woman who was obviously with them. She offered to let us to give some milk to a baby tiger, which Marc did.

Again, this was quite an unforgettable experience that you don't get to do in many places. The baby tiger was not that small really, about the size of a big dog. I guess that was quite commercialised, but it still had some Eden-like magic about it all. Marc did feel the paws on his arms, but enjoyed the whole experience. This was the end of a beautiful long weekend, and I was looking forward to seeing Allan and Vivienne again after quite some time away from each other; I was also looking forward to more travelling with a great sense of freedom for myself.

Northern Italy

END AUGUST 2006

As we were back in Europe and had been invited to my French niece's wedding in Italy – the bridegroom being from Turin – we thought we might as well take advantage of the invitation there to grab a one week holiday in Italy again. And so we were able to have our last holiday with our daughter Vivienne before she went off and left our home in the UK.

Before the actual wedding, we visited beautiful old Turin, a very smart place with graceful buildings everywhere.

The place was enchanting with all the red roofs showing how well preserved it was, perhaps enriched by the fact that it had held the Olympic Games in the winter.

There were even some pretty well preserved ruins which were over 2,000 years old. It was quite incredible to see all this beauty in just this one town, and we just had to marvel at such a rich history. This is perhaps why Italy always seemed to invite us back again and again to discover yet more gems, and we still have not seen half of this magical country. It never ceases to surprise us and entice us.

The old town of Turin was even more magical and full of charm, very coquettish and pretty, incredibly attractive and a delight to wander around – an even older part of an already old city, very quaint and unexpected. It felt like a town built for fairytales, and out of this world. Turin did indeed have a few surprises and I never expected such beauty and variety within what is, after all, quite a big city and more famous for its manufacture of Fiats rather than its architecture, but I was pleasantly surprised.

Then it was time to meet up with my family in a small village not far from Turin, right in the mountains, with some chalets around and the skiing tracks; this was where the Winter Olympics actually happened.

The little village had its curiosities too, in the shape of extremely old housing with old tiles looking as if they were going to fall any time, and beautifully decorated chalets with traditional shutters and flowers overhanging them.

The wedding day arrived with the bride and bridegroom beautifully clothed in creamy outfits in a horse carriage matching the pretty area; some accordions played and there were folk dances outside followed by dinner in a friendly atmosphere.

The weather was quite cool due to the proximity of the mountains, but still fun was had by all and I was glad we were back in Europe to be able to enjoy this wedding.

We would not have been able to attend if we had stayed in Australia; it came at the right time especially when we consider that we were going to go back to Australia only a year later, earlier than expected. For the time being we were just going to concentrate on this wedding in the beautiful surroundings with family, which is quite a rare occasion nowadays.

Here are more photographs of this great day and another day of celebration the next day, after which we stayed in accommodation in various chalets around the area before setting off to go and visit family near Milan and gorgeous Bardi (close to Bore, where Allan's mother was from).

We met up again with Allan's family in and around Bore, although Bardi is scenically the highlight of the area, prettier and more animated than its neighbour, with its castle dominating the town. Then we saw the house built by Allan's grandfather, saw his aunt Anna again and various cousins, and went for some walks in the mountains. In these mountains, I felt quite young despite soon reaching half a century, which seemed like a grand old age. But I did not allow myself to be fazed by it and have decided to enjoy life as it should be, as advised by my mother – advice which is so very wise. But where have all the years gone I wonder….

It was quite touching meeting up with Allan' s Italian family again and seeing this part of the world where his mother grew up before leaving for the UK at the tender age of eighteen. Here is a set of various photographs taken at random from the album before finishing this break. I wanted to capture the beautiful town of Bardi, and also Allan's Italian family who we had met a few times before both in the UK and in Italy. We probably wouldn't be able to see again for quite a while, due to distance and circumstances, and also the time when I became fifty or close to it.

Living in the UK meant every European country was close by and fairly easy to reach and we decided to take advantage of that as we were going to return to Australia and far away shores, which allowed for future visits in Southeast Asia.

For the time being we were enjoying once again beautiful Italy, which never disappointed us. Wherever we went there were architectural treasures to be discovered, and it is a country on par with France – my home country, to be honest. These are a lot of pictures of myself because Allan is usually the photographer with the eye for the picture. ♀

Berlin, Dresden and Prague

END DECEMBER 2006 TO BEGINNING JANUARY 2007

This time, we decided to go on holidays for a week in the middle of winter, and in cold places for once, and spent a week visiting Berlin where my niece and two friends of mine lived. We also visited Dresden – which I knew was quite an impressive city even though some of it had been destroyed during the Second World War – and then Prague, famous for its beautiful architecture.

We first headed for Berlin right after Christmas; my friend Waltraut had left her flat right in the middle of the city for us while she was on holiday to some sunnier climates, but we were to see her again at the end of our trip back in Berlin for the New Year. So we gratefully accepted her offer of accommodation in a very stately-looking one bedroom flat with very high ceilings, very well placed in a nice area.

Waltraut had left some lovely 'christmasy' decorations and chocolates for us nicely displayed on the table, so this was a nice surprise to welcome us.

The following day, we set off to visit the centre of Berlin with the Brandenburg Gate, the museum, and the Christmas markets, so fairy-like with tons of lights brimming with joy draped over the trees and a huge Christmas tree. Allan went down a snowy slope on a huge tyre, having fun. It was very cold and rainy, but the warm chestnuts at the various Christmas stands warmed us up and it was very atmospheric; there were loads of people celebrating New Year's Eve and it was becoming more and more crowded, so we eventually retired to the flat.

We met up with my old friend Jurgen in a café near the old Berlin Wall. The café's decor depicted scenes when the Berlin wall still existed – the infamous wall separating West Berlin from the poorer East and separating so many families; and when it went down, it caused so much joy.

We bought a little piece of the stone from the infamous wall which had caused so much misery after the Second World War; a punishment for a strong Germany which had provoked two world wars in the same century and meant to weaken the country. I will always remember the sad words of Jurgen in the past saying how ashamed he was of being German, but this was not his fault -- a war waged by previous generations which had nothing to do with him. He was a very peaceful soul.

We had a long walk around some of the parts of the wall which had remained a testimony to history, a grey sad looking wall which I prefer not to scan; instead, here is a picture of a lovely Christmas scene very cleverly achieved with some white tents surrounding the great buildings and a Christmas tree, looking very cold indeed. It was not snowing, but felt cold enough for snow.

We left Berlin for imposing Dresden with its big impressive buildings; they all looked enormous, seeming to say, "You tried to destroy me but I am indestructible. Look how grand I am". We walked up lots of stairs to have a view over the city and I was quite exhausted at the end of the walk, but it was worth it in the end.

We walked past what must have been a hotel, which contrasted with the grand, darker buildings typical of Dresden, to discover a lovely pastel-coloured place with a lot of charm. It looked more like a palace and not so much like a fortress, which made a nice change from the sterner Dresden we had seen so far.

This is not a criticism, as Dresden was much more impressive than I had thought it would be. There I found a nice dark green short coat, warmer than my other jacket and much needed for this very cold climate. This was a bit of a shock after hot Australia with even its winters being fairly mild, and we were rosy from the cold. Dresden had been a charming city full of culture where we could easily have attended some great concerts, no doubt; the high street shopping was of the highest quality and at fairly decent prices as well. It was a more compact city than Berlin, and quite a different place altogether. So I was pleased I had put Dresden on our week-long itinerary, and the train to get there made it very accessible as well.

Our next destination before returning to Berlin for the flight back to the UK was the very famous Prague, a jewel of a place which I could not wait to visit, having heard so much about it. It did not disappoint, despite our arrival at the station being interrupted by loud shouts of 'There is a dangerous criminal on the loose around the place'. This was quite scary and we left this seedy area by tube to reach the much nicer city centre. Everywhere you looked there were some gorgeous buildings, one after the other. I did not know where to look, being literally surrounded by magnificent buildings rivalling each other, the cobbled streets adding to its undeniable charms. The town was full of people warmly wrapped against the bitter cold as we were in the middle of winter. Nothing was out of place, and it looked built for a magical world, almost unreal down to the car in the photograph above.

The interior of the pretty churches were mostly in the baroque style, adding to the cheerfulness of the place, even in the middle of winter.

The buildings were joyfully surrounding us with their bright colours and their delicate bells; the clock of the most famous building in the middle of the street chiming with abandon every so often; the octagonal shapes adding to the magical atmosphere; the beautiful Charles Bridge linking one area to the other one with the huge castle area on the other side. There was also a very cute area of low Hansel and Gretel-like houses in an area called Zlata Ulicka. This place had so much to offer to visitors, you could not help but be mesmerised by it all.

At last, it was time to leave this enchanting city to take the train back to Berlin, where we would be able to see Waltraut, back from her trip overseas, and also my niece and her husband and daughter for dinner in their flat. It was good to see both sets of people before returning once again to the UK before our next adventure. Germany was going to be a saviour as far as my health was concerned, and I will forever owe a debt to Germany. Despite the bitterly cold weather, we had a great winter break. The great advantage of Europe is that so many countries which are so different from each other are at your front door, ready to be explored. We have visited a lot of places in Europe over the years, but there are still many which we have not visited. Such a big and such a small world at the same time!

A WEEK IN

New York and Boston

MARCH 2007

As our eldest son Jim was now living in New York and we were back in the UK, we decided we might as well pay him a visit there and see him in his new element, and at the same time visit our American cousins in Boston whom we had not seen since leaving good old Texas all those years before.

As I am writing this, I can see our life flashing by, the interesting turns it took, and how time flies.

The first thing we did was head straight to our son's flat in New York City from where we were going to visit Central Park and the surrounding neighbourhoods under the blue, cold early-spring sky. I had forgotten that the beige buildings near the park were quite elegant despite their height, and not the empty hard lines of new skyscrapers which keep mushrooming everywhere nowadays to my dismay. These had some lovely towers with delicate roofs, but of course the new glass-like ones were there too like a big concrete jungle surrounding the even bigger green 'jungle' of the park, which was the lung of the city which never sleeps.

It was great to have the Coombes family together (apart from Vivienne) as this had become quite a rarity lately, and all the sadder for it really. To live miles away had its advantages but also its disadvantages, and this was one of them. It was a pleasure to see Marc reunited with his big brother, who obviously cared a lot for him. The day was quite cool and a brisk walk in the park pleasantly warmed us; it felt quite atmospheric, unique to New York. There were horse carriages parked at the entrance; again these were quite unique and hopefully they will stay – a great and romantic way of wandering around Central Park via vehicles from a bygone era. We did not take them and preferred our own two feet, but could not help admiring them.

We reluctantly left Central Park to go and visit the famous MoMA, which had some very impressive paintings by Monet and many other artists; this is perhaps the museum not to miss if you only have a short time in New York.

After this great visit, Jim took us to his place of work with the BNP and showed us where he sat when at work. It was great to have an insight into his work place, and be able to imagine him working there when we would be so far away from him. He seemed much at ease and in his element, at least at that time in life.

The next day saw us walking on Broadway, famous for its theatres. It was boldly exhuming its uniqueness, and the sky that day was a perfect cold blue which added to its vibrancy. Since we were having an arts day, Jim took us next to the other famous museum, the Guggenheim. Its exterior was pretty unusual, like the beige peel of a potato or an apple with different layers and rounded with some portholes in various places. Inside, we went up a spiral staircase looking at the mostly Spanish paintings, which were showcased that day. I must say I preferred the MoMA with regards to the paintings, but this building was worth visiting for its own sake.

We were then back among the huge buildings and had to crane our necks to see their heights; we went up Rockefeller Centre to have a plunging view over Central Park, stretching for miles below. The high needle of the Empire State Building dominating the high-rise was still elegant. This was well after the Twin Towers had been sadly destroyed on 11th September 2001, not so long ago and still vivid in most people's memory, but we did see the remnants of what was left there – Ground Zero – on our way back to the city after having visited our good friends on the outskirts of New York and Allan's cousins in Boston. It was soon time to leave Jim for a while to catch our train at beautiful Grand Central Station, which did deserve its title and was indeed a very grand place – what a station should be like.

The train took us to Old Greenwich where our good old friends Linda and David lived, friends from way back when they also used to live in Claygate. Linda was Marc's godmother and they had moved to New York quite a few years before after we had returned from Texas, but their move there was a permanent one.

It was wonderful seeing them again after so many years, and they had not changed; well, David had gone grey (but as women we disguise this more easily and it looks much better on a man) and wore a beard. We had a picnic by the beach not far from their beautiful house, where we stayed for a couple of nights. We chatted away like in the good old days, no difference whatsoever. Their house was gorgeous and typically American with white wood, a huge veranda, and shutters to protect from the bitter cold days that New York can have and the also very hot and humid days in the summer.

The days seemed to have become much milder since we had arrived, and indeed very spring-like when they took us to the long beach accompanied by their gorgeous little dog. They took us to a super Japanese restaurant in the evening with their children where the chef cooked right in front of us.

We'd had a great time and it was again reluctantly and sadly that we said our goodbyes – when were we going to see them again? As I am writing this, we still have not, but we have kept in touch via email and also once with Skype – which brought us close as if we were next door, and that felt quite emotional.

We went back to New York City before leaving for Boston and took the opportunity to visit what we had not been able to before, including the tragic Ground Zero where over three thousand people had died in the Twin Towers – a symbol of American power and capitalism. It felt very sad, even more so as we had gone up those towers on our last visit on the way back from San Antonio. It felt like a cataclysm had come and gone, and you wonder how some people could have such evil in them, destroying the lives of so many innocent people.

Another quick tour took us around the city, close to the American Stock Exchange, and we took the free boat to Staten Island around the Statue of Liberty which had been given to America by France, but no one could disembark on the island due to security and there were US Coast Guards permanently going round on their high speed boats. The weather had taken a turn for the worse, and indeed it snowed. The cars around Jim's flat were covered by a layer of 2 cm of snow, quite a surprise after the mild time we had experienced while with Linda and David.

We had to make do with it and took the Amtrak train to our next destination, Providence in Rhode Island not far from Boston. Because of the snow, we were not able to visit Boston again this time. Evelyn and Francis's house was very warm and well insulated thankfully, and she had lovely food prepared for us. Their house was lovely too and looked almost fairy-like. It seemed to come straight out of the Little Red Riding Hood book, with all the woods around and its almost complete isolation in the middle of nowhere. That first evening, we had a great game of dominoes – different American dominoes which were much more interesting, and which they were generous to buy for us later on.

We then went to our respective bedrooms; ours was beautiful with a four poster bed, and we slept soundly in this gorgeous house.

The next day, we ventured outside in the by now very deep snow; we borrowed scarves, gloves, and hats and had a good time experiencing snow the likes of which I had not seen for a long time, but it was quite fitting in this area, and not out of place at all. We did not stay very long but it was nice to have some fresh air in the snow.

Afterwards, as it seemed the roads were all right to drive on, Evelyn and Francis took us to see his Mum, Esther, who was by then ninety-one years old and who still lived in her own house. However, I think the children now did her shopping. As I remember she was only complaining about a bad knee, not bad for that age; I hope I can grow that old looking so well and cheerful, alert and with only a bad knee! We saw the lovely Capitol-like building of the City Hall by the station in the town of Providence.

It was time to leave the cousins and head back to New York where Jim made us meet his girlfriend Dominique – half Swedish, half French – that he had met in a restaurant, so it was fitting that we all went to a restaurant for our last night in the States before going back to the UK. We eventually found one that pleased Allan, where we could hear ourselves talking.

Central France and South of France

AUGUST 2007

This time round, we did not go too far and not for very long, due to a hip resurfacing operation I had in Germany in July –hence my big debt to Germany. I was fit and healthy yet again, and back on the road a month later, first of all to go to my nephew's wedding in central France near Nevers, where one of my brothers lived. So it was wedding time in France for my family, and since we were there anyway, we decided to take advantage of the situation and from there go spend a few days in the south of France in an area I did not know yet, where we would be able to have some sunshine again.

For the first time in a long time, I was able to be with my three brothers, Michel, Jacques, and Christian once again, a rare occasion. It was great to be surrounded by my dear brothers again after so long. Christian had prepared lovely food for all the family who had come before the actual wedding, and we had a lovely tour of his great garden (his pride and joy), with beautiful healthy vegetables such as pumpkin, and plants growing in abundance. He was an expert in gardening and farming and it showed. We took a picture of his huge sunflowers towering over us; I had never seen such huge sunflowers in my life before.

This garden was like a mini paradise with all those gorgeous flowers and with vivid colours sprouting everywhere. The next day that we had before the wedding, Christian took us to a gorgeous *village de France* not far from their house. We stayed in some of the pretty, small houses which included a bedroom and a bathroom, and had been converted into mini-bed and breakfast housing for the students' families who came to the agricultural school where my brother worked.

This little village was built out of a creamy stone with well rounded hedges around it, brown shutters and with red roofs, all in a similar style exuding a calm atmosphere.

People living there were renting the houses and obviously took pleasure in their environment. There were some mansions which were more like castles, but these were inhabited too. We did not have time to visit Nevers but the very little I saw of it was rather nice with medieval streets, something I did not expect and hope to visit one day as I only had a glimpse from the train station where we had been picked up.

Then it was time for a nice dinner, all organised by my brother yet again, and Marc enjoyed the watermelon that was served at the end – most likely from Christian's garden, natural and tasty.

Then came a lovely couple of days, starting with the actual wedding with the beige pastel colours, looking quite smart on a nice sunny day. They were lucky as the days before had been greyer, but the sun had deigned to come out for their day.

It was good seeing my sister-in-law's family; all her three sisters were there, my other nieces who I had not seen for a while, as well as the aging but still quite vibrant parents of my sister-in-law, Annie. I know these photos are not an actual part of the holiday, but since it started like the other one in Italy, I thought it was worth including them in this book.

We left extended family behind and went on the next part of our little jaunt; since we were already part of the way to the south of France, it seemed like a good idea to visit some more of it. The three of us took the train to Nîmes, well known for its arenas dating from 2,000 years ago, and they were indeed quite fascinating. The whole town was very interesting and vestiges of Roman times were to be found here and there as the Romans did indeed come to Nîmes and this region and built those magnificent buildings that we can still admire today.

We rented a car to visit some of the places, and stayed in some small hotels which we found there and then. Our next port of call was Aiguemortes with its canals and the great old town where we had a lovely walk; from its heights, we could see the red roofs so typical of the south of France or Italy that I love so much.

The whole area was a delight to the eyes, from the beautiful towns we visited to the lovely Camargue area, with its flamingos which had migrated from Africa to this enchanting and still quite wild area for the summer. It was good to experience some of the countryside for a change in the delightful warmth; I posed by a lovely house with shutters typical of the south of France, thinking this would be a nice place to have; the sort of dream place I always wanted to buy, which I might realise one day.

After this great day, we visited the medieval town of les Beaux de Provence, with its narrow steep alleys, little shops full of curios, and cafes dominated by the ruins of its fortress-like castle which must have seen some wars during the Middle Ages. The weather had gone much cooler, but that did not last. It was a very quaint town, and one of the most visited in the area.

The area was full of famous vineyards, Chateau Neuf du Pape being one of them, and we travelled around it. Here again were more vestiges dating from at least the Middle Ages, and we made a stopover right at the top overlooking the gorgeous scenery below. The weather had turned nice again thank goodness; this was the south of France, after all, and the weather at that time never stayed dull for very long. I had not realised how pretty this area was and was most impressed. So far, I only knew the area around Nice in the south of France, but everywhere there seemed some place worth visiting and somewhere where I might one day put my suitcases down. This would be only for a little while, as I believe my thirst for travelling would still push me to visit other places in the world, but this certainly could be somewhere to relax for a few months every year – who knows?

Next on our itinerary was the imposing town of Avignon, with the huge Palais des Papes where the popes used to reside before choosing Rome. This palace was most impressive and attracted a high number of tourists. We did not visit inside but the view of the outside was just incredible, and it stood proud over the town and above its famous unfinished bridge.

Last on our trip, we had to see the most famously well-preserved Pont du Gard. Again dating back 2,000 years, the whole structure was simply amazing. We did visit Arles quickly, but somehow were not particularly impressed; we should probably visit another time as I believe we would and should have been more impressed by this town, so famous because of Van Gogh.

Still, on the whole, we had been enchanted by our trip to the south of France and I was pleased that I walked well and mostly without the crutches that I was hiding behind me in photographs but hardly using any more. It reminded me how my home country has so much to offer and so much variety; on all my trips abroad I tend to forget this, and I was glad to share some of my country with my husband and youngest son.

Vanuatu

28TH SEPTEMBER TO 6TH OCTOBER 2008

We left the UK once again in October to join Allan who, in September, had gone back to Australia for work yet again, this time in Brisbane. I was not too keen to come back, but everything seemed to draw us back here including, for Allan, a need to return to his beloved Australia. We had done some more visiting around Brisbane and a long weekend around Bundaberg to see the turtles laying their eggs etc., and we needed some more holidays. Therefore we chose to spend a week in Vanuatu, an island not so far away from Brisbane, in the Pacific. We only had a week, but the place was enchanting and gave us a sense of adventure.

We had some problem with Marc's passport when we arrived as his visa had expired, making me realise that I needed to make sure he had an Australian passport for such visits in the future. We arrived by taxi to the house I had booked for a few days. It was a lovely, big place with a wonderful garden where everything seemed to be growing including grapefruit, almonds, and great tropical flowers. We could walk from there to the centre of Port Vila, not far away but a little bit run down with some cafes and restaurants which were rather expensive when you consider this was a Third World island. So we decided to buy some food for our dinner and breakfast and the next evening Anastasia, our host, was going to cook some speciality of the island for us, and this was going to give us much laughter. The fairly dumpy town made me aware that Allan could be right about colonial powers staying longer in such places until they could cope for themselves.

After our breakfast of bread and jam, cereals, and coffee/tea, we had some time to spend in the garden and I even found a hammock to laze about in before we went to see the new cathedral further from the city centre, in an area that was actually livelier and probably the actual centre of the town. This area had a nicer feel about it and we reached the Australian embassy to sort out Marc's problem, but were told it was too late and we would have had to come the next day. We went to visit the museum and had a drink nearby where we met the café's boss, an Australian man who had made a fortune here. The museum was very interesting and showed Vanuatu's history; Vanuatu had been under French rule alongside British rule – this was most unusual but it worked. In 1990 the island became independent, and poorer and poorer from what we could see. The people there were a very friendly people however, despite their poverty.

We decided to go to nearby Isiki Island and headed back to the more dumpy part of town, but unfortunately the free ferry to reach the island did not exist anymore. We should have had to pay quite a big sum just for the pleasure of a ten minute crossing (and redeem some restaurant voucher on the other side), but we could already imagine the cost of these restaurants which were just for the tourists in what was actually a resort on the other island.

So instead, we decided to take a boat with the locals for a much more reasonable price, and it was fun. Everything on that island was well looked after and beautifully paved. There was a small beach and some pools attached to the resort, but it all looked really artificial and empty of life apart from a few people looking bored by the poolside and a guard asking us if we stayed on the resort, but he let us stay for a bit longer. I could just not grasp the point of coming here and just being with other Australians by a pool – there was no point at all. Especially when we had, in a way, our own resort back at our house in Brisbane, as did many other Australians! So we went back to the ferry and crossed on the local boat once again, and we were glad to be in the real Vanuatu, never mind if it was a little bit rundown. We strolled to the fascinating market, and drank some coconut milk straight from the coconut before returning to 'our' house.

At the house, our host Anastasia, who was actually the maid of people who were living in New Caledonia, had a lap-lap ready for us – a really interesting meal consisting of chicken with yams and tomatoes and other vegetables in delicious coconut milk sauce, wrapped in some banana leaves alongside a refreshing salad of cucumber in coconut and lemon. It was quite delicious. We had dinner with her, her little boy, and her niece. They spoke French – people on this island seemed to speak either French or English. We talked about various things such as education, and this was a surprise: it was not free, and they had to pay $50 a term which, for them, was quite a lot. This meant that a lot of people there could not afford to stay at school, generally left at age 12, and then hung about in the streets as we had seen in Port Vila, by the sea and restaurants. Anastasia claimed that life in Vanuatu was better under the French when school had been free. There were no unemployment benefits now, and it made me angry thinking about school children in the west who have access to free education at least until the age of 18 and mess about in class!

We went back to the Australian embassy the next day to finally sort out Marc's passport problem and make sure he could come back with us to Brisbane!

Then we took a minibus to the Melemele waterfalls, passing some interesting hamlets on the way, where we could not help but notice that some people lived in terrible shacks – reminding us that we were indeed in a third world island – while we also went past a golf club, the total opposite to the local poverty. We had to change our shoes as we had to cross some water in places to reach the waterfalls and it started raining quite heavily, so we used some huge banana leaves which were all around us as umbrellas, and it helped. The day had started too hot and there were some little turquoise 'ponds' and water gurgling over steps; this was the point where I had to stop, as it could have been too dangerous in case I slipped and undid the great work the surgeon did on my hip. Allan and Marc went on and managed to go under the waterfall for a swim.

We then walked back and stopped along the road to find the 'Secret Garden'; we stopped en route at a little store where we bought some ice cream and some bread as we only had a packet of biscuits with us. We paid the lady at the entrance of this open air museum, and found that she was married to an Englishman. The place was very interesting and in a lovely outside setting; lots of things were written on trees regarding the past – the customs, the colonisers, circumcision, the various plants and ... cannibalism! The last act of cannibalism was in Malekula Island, where our host originated from, and happened in 1969, not so long ago. Apparently, human flesh was consumed in yams with coconut, which was the type of food we'd had yesterday apart from the source of the meat – which was quite interesting! We saw how the famous 'kava', a strong alcohol, was made and Allan had a cup of that; it was supposed to make you peaceful. We then took another minibus back to Port Vila passing by the village of Mele, which was quite an amazing place with pigs roaming around and which had women in lovely flowered dresses in front of their corrugated houses. There were also a couple of nice houses right in the middle of the shacks.

The following day saw us getting up quite late to catch another minibus to Hideaway Island this time, then a ferry to the actual island itself. We had to pay an entrance fee there and hire some snorkelling gear for Marc while I just had a bit of a swim in the sea with coral under my feet, but it was nice to lie by the sea and have my feet licked by the sweet warm water – definitely warmer than the sea in Australia. We were lucky with the weather, and Allan and Marc went snorkelling and marvelled at the lovely fish around them. I walked around the small island and found a lovely little beach all to myself away from the café and other people. We had to take the boat back at 4.30 pm, and strolled on the beach on the other side of this little island, a long beach where unfortunately a lot of ground was being sold to mainly New Zealanders, from what we were told later.

Finally back at 'our' nice retreat, Anastasia had another meal ready for us – a free meal this time as we had paid for the meal the day before. This time it was vine leaves with minced meat and cabbage and manioc grated together as a salad, which was very nice indeed. She even gave a present to Marc, but it was made from straw and we would never be able to go through customs back in Australia with it. It was a shame as it was rather nice.

We met an Australian girl married to some person from Guadeloupe at the post office and they lived on the island with their kid, planning on going to Guadeloupe in the future – a place I would love to visit one day. So many places to see and so little time! We booked ourselves a taxi for the next day to take us up to the north of the island where we could get to another not very well known little island called N'Guna Island. The next day we would have to pack and leave the house, which I could only book until that time as other people had booked it for later on; but it served its purpose and allowed us to go to this little island and stay there overnight.

The road the next day started fine, but quickly became very bumpy as it was unpaved for quite a lot of the way, and there were people walking on the road seemingly going nowhere. The road was being constructed and this would probably change the whole area, and our secret little island. The scenery was lovely with many trees, and huge tall palm trees gently moved in the light wind, sometimes opening onto vistas of the blue sea. We stopped at a village where there were a number of WWII objects, and even a tank by the sea which was all rusted. Suddenly we had come to the end of the road at a small pier and while we waited for the small boat which was going to take us the N'Guna Island, we had our picnic in the shade while picking up some lovely shells at the same time – there were huge clam shells all around. The motorboat arrived and took us quickly to the island; we had the company of a young American woman. Her name was Tina and we were going to stay in touch with her from that time; in fact, as I am writing this I am still in contact with her in the States.

Someone arrived on the beach from nowhere to take our luggage and bring us to their bungalows, which we rented for the decent price of 3,000 vatus per person, including all meals. The conditions were quite primitive without electricity or water, and toilets outside; we basically had a thatched hut for the two of us, and another one for Marc, and we had to sleep with a mosquito net. Actually it was quite romantic, and I felt like Robinson Crusoe. It was only for two nights and we actually enjoyed this unforgettable experience; there were only the four of us tourists on this island and it felt like a privilege, away from the grumpy resort tourists who did not even greet us with a hello.

We soon had a nice 'salady' meal after our walk on the path, and we met up with Tina for a short while as she was staying in another place not far away. We went to bed quite early in our hut by the beach.

We woke up the next day after quite a good night's sleep to find our breakfast already made in another hut even closer to the beach; we had some really nice bread, other cakes, and juice, and it was rather delicious. Afterwards, we met up with Tina to go for a walk with a guide, and we walked to the 300 year old banyan tree through the forest and diverse plantations of yams, coconut trees, manioc, pineapples, banana trees and mango trees, and then back to the village via a church with a huge mango tree next to it. En route, we saw some pigs and piglets (they are a symbol of how well-off people are, and are very important there) and a craft shop. The whole village was very tidy and everyone greeted us; it was a lovely walk. Then it was back to our hut by the sea for lunch followed by a walk on the sandy beach with only Allan brave enough to go in the sea, where he snorkelled – the wind had become very strong and brisk. We walked right to the end where there were many huge black volcanic rocks, and we met some kids coming back from school to whom we chatted in English. These kids were very bright and loved school; what a difference from British and Australian kids. I would have taught these with pleasure.

Then a larger group of teenagers arrived on the beach and they definitely looked more threatening, I believe one of them had a knife as well. Oh well, after all, this was where the first Presbyterian minister had come in 1870 and only escaped the cooking pot because he was so charismatic, but this showed us that these people were descended from cannibals, which made us feel a chill and get away from the group quickly.

We had a nice meal in our hut yet again, and I felt I could get used to this life – no cooking, no shopping, quite ideal. The cook was excellent and we'd had a great, unusual day in an unspoilt place in our little unknown paradise – something we had not experienced yet. We had to get up early the next day to catch the boat just after 6.15 am. I did not sleep well as I was getting worried about the strong wind, but it had abated by the time we took the boat. We had another great breakfast of yummy fried bananas with other things before leaving.

The colours of this place are something quite incredible; the whole place is brimming with riotous and yet peaceful colours, and there is no doubt you are in the tropics there! We met a little girl and another lady. The little 9-year-old girl was very sweet and was going to visit her Mum in Port Vila.

The boat stopped en route at Pele Island, another place which looked very nice, and this time we took the truck back to the capital, leaving Tina behind as she was staying one more day on the island. The truck was cheaper and actually quicker than the taxi had been. Marc remembered that we had seen Tina (but not spoken to her) on the island where he and Allan had been snorkelling.

At around 9 am we were in our new hotel, which I had booked on the Internet in Brisbane. The owner had thought it was just the two of us, so for the first night we had a double bed and an extra mattress, but due to this, we had a free breakfast the next day on the veranda where we talked to a young and friendly French couple. We had a walk back to the town centre to buy a lovely French cake from a cake shop we had discovered called the *péché mignon* – the cute sin. These cakes were proper French cakes and most delicious, accompanied by a fruit juice. We also bought some huge sandwiches for later. Pity we had not discovered this place earlier!

Next we headed to Erakor Island by minibus and boat. The beaches there were not so good and were hurting our feet, but the water was shallow and we had a rest. We met some unfriendly Australians who did not even greet us – where was N'Guna? It seemed like a lovely way of life there but, of course, you have to wonder whether you would be bored if you actually lived there! We had a picnic on the beach, went back to Port Vila, and left Marc in the hotel, going to a pub for a short time by ourselves.

The next day was our last full day in Vanuatu and we had our usual nice breakfast of egg on toast, bread and jam, mango and papaya juice, tea/coffee/milk, cereals – rather nice! We chatted again with the young French couple from Avignon and to a German lady who had been travelling around the islands with someone on her catamaran for a few months, a rather exciting way of travelling if you can do it. She mentioned the volcanic island of Tanna where I would have liked to go and where you could feel the ground literally move under your feet: it is the most accessible active volcano in the world. It was a shame that we did not have enough time to go there and I would like to go back to Vanuatu to do this and perhaps stay on another island instead. We bargained with a taxi to take us to Eton's blue lagoon and Eton's Beach. The blue lagoon was opened especially for us – a lovely blue hole with perfectly clear water and beautiful flowers all around. We went with the owner in his canoe, a traditional wooden one. This was the perfect place to do this, and I managed to see those lovely fishes I had missed while on Hideaway Island; you could see them with the naked eye, so clear was the water! Allan swam in the lagoon which eventually went to the sea, and we had a picnic there and walked to the beach a kilometre or so further on.

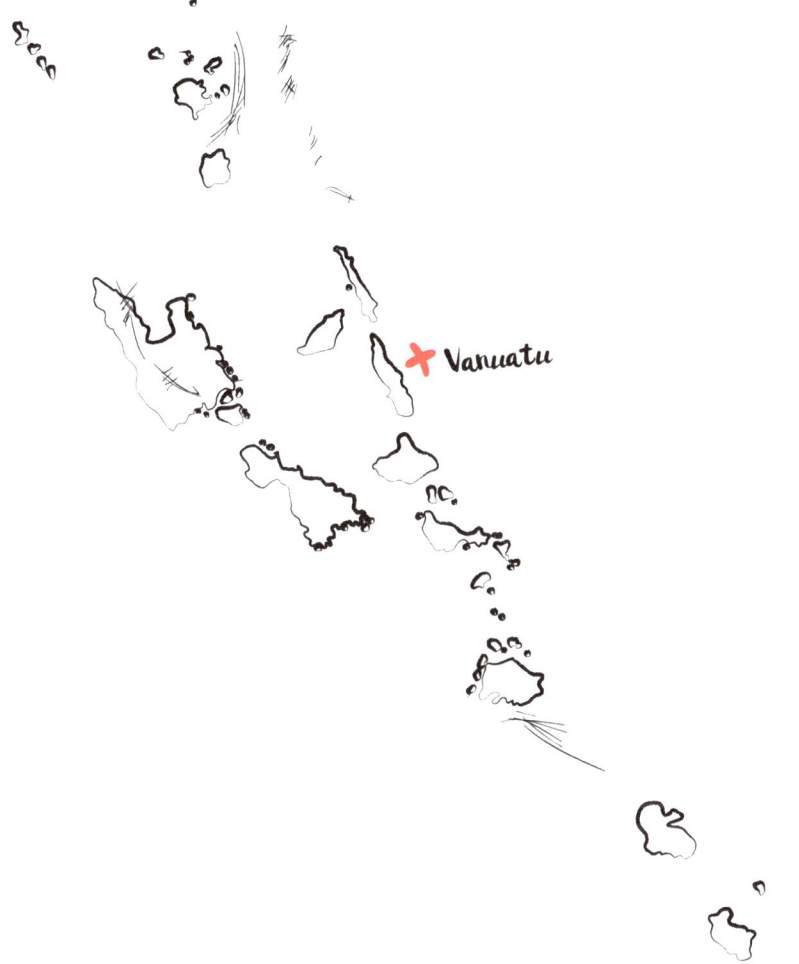

By that time, the sky had turned grey and the sea was pretty rough. We met a young couple from New Caledonia, and while she was pleasant he was not and did not want their photograph taken when we offered to do so – oh well, it takes all sorts I suppose. We then drove back to Port Vila for a game of cards and dinner; it was raining by then, but I think we had been fairly lucky with the weather on the whole.

I will always remember the tiny island where we stayed with Tina, who later on dropped her huge luggage with us in Brisbane to go and explore more of Southeast Asia. She had been studying for six months on the Gold Coast and was very brave to do all this on her own. She came to retrieve her heavy bag later on and stayed with us overnight. As I said, we have been in touch ever since and hopefully I will visit her one day in the States. I will also always remember the vivid colours of that tropical island and the smiles of the young children. It was a different type of trip altogether!

North America

DECEMBER 2008 TO JANUARY 2009

We had saved the longest holiday to go and visit Jim in the USA, and left Brisbane on December 24th to travel there via Japan. Due to the time difference, we were able to have two Christmas Eves on this holiday, the first one in Tokyo, where it was quite cold and where we had quite a few hours to be able to visit Narita, the city next to the airport which had a number of things of interest. Narita was a very pretty, authentic place with many temples and narrow streets – quite a little jewel next to the huge megalopolis which was Tokyo.

After having a really nice time in Narita – a lovely way to start the Christmas holidays – we were on a plane again, and reached Los Angeles a few hours later. We were pretty tired by the time the plane arrived and booked a taxi to go to the lovely artist's place we had booked for about ten days, and it did not disappoint. We slept for hours on end in the big room, which had been cleverly split up into various living areas. It was very comfortable with a high double bed and another smaller one for Marc on the other side of the bedroom, a lounge area, and another space for the dining room. There were some beautiful orange trees that you could see through the back window of our rented house on Venice Beach. This was a home from home, and at a very decent price.

The next day, Jim arrived with his wife Dominique and brought us a hamper of food as they were going to spend the day with her parents, whom we had been invited to have lunch with on the 26th. We opened our presents from them, including a great book about France for me. It was nice to see our Jim again on Christmas Day, even though it was only for a short time, but we were going to spend quite a few days with him anyway before heading back on the road again. This was again not a real backpacking trip, but an independent trip nevertheless mixed with visiting family. Christmas Day, the three of us had a simple meal before setting out for a walk in the area; it was pretty cold here too, and we walked right to the beach and were able to have a look at Santa Monica. In the evening we watched some TV back at the house.

On Boxing Day, Jim and his wife came to pick us up to go to her parents' house, not far from Hollywood and close to Beverly Hills. The dad was French and much older than us, and the mother had been a model – she was blonde and smartly dressed, and originally from Sweden.

We had a lovely meal with some delicious ham and various vegetables, followed by dessert and were fuller than the day before with our frugal Christmas meal.

The following day, the three of us went by bus to the famous and free Getty Museum, which had been given to the city by J. Paul Getty himself so that everyone could appreciate the arts free of charge – a very charming idea! The whole place was quite fascinating not just because of its art but also because of its very interesting architecture and gardens, and we spent a great day there.

It was quite a cold day, but we saw a fantastic sunset – nature's way of telling us that it could beat the beauty of the Getty Museum or any manmade building any time. Fabulous orange sheets were draping the sky with incandescent light while the pale yellow part of the sun gently retreated behind the hill; this incredible sunset shone on a huge sculpture and its tender gold brown leaves, enhancing the statue's beauty.

Next, it was off to Santa Monica for the evening with its famous wheel on its pier, radiating into the night. The next day, Jim came with us on his own to go and visit the famous Universal Studios with all its crazy signs, rides, and stunt cars; there was a reproduction of the shark from *Jaws* which had been used in the films, a lovely huge fairy-like creamy teapot with artificial Christmas trees dusted with false snow, and a prettified false street reminding us of Europe, which had been used in an American television series. The place was pretty special and well situated in the heights behind Los Angeles, and we spent the whole day there. It was fun for everyone and at not too bad a price considering all the special effects we could experience. I also remember that the price for a whole year would have cost local residents only one dollar extra, so that was quite a good deal if you lived in Los Angeles and had visitors, as this was certainly a place not to miss. The day also allowed us to have a nice chat with our eldest son in freedom, a privilege these days.

The next day, Dominique's mother drove us to the city centre past Mexican areas which were pretty lively, and a more touristy Mexican area where we had a walk in its old quarter. We visited the City Hall and the modern cultural centre which had some very interesting round silver shapes, and then drove back to Hollywood where we saw the pink stars with the names of the famous actors inscribed on them all along the pavement. Los Angeles is a very interesting city and we did take the bus a couple of times to the centre, although it was not recommended; it is usually the poorer people who catch the bus in American cities but this did not stop us, and the buses were actually quite reliable.

We only had one more day left with Jim and after having watched some TV on New Year's Eve, we were able to actually have New Year's Day with him and Dominique. We went to celebrate in a Mexican restaurant on Venice Beach, in an area quite removed from where we were and that we did not know, close to many little boats anchored in the Marina del Rey Bay. This was quite a picturesque area in which to have our last day with Jim before he headed off with his wife's family to some reunion somewhere in the mountains near Palm Springs, where we ourselves were going to head later on during our journey. It felt quite sad having to leave him, not knowing when we would see him again after having been able to spend a few days with him. I do wish the two brothers could see more of each other, and hopefully this will happen in the future.

On the second of January, Allan wanted to do some work on some grant application that he had to do on a regular basis, so Marc and I went off on our own to go and visit UCLA, one of the most famous universities in Los Angeles. The buildings had gorgeous 'orangy' bricks, and it was in a nice setting. We then had our last day in the area visiting pretty Pasadena in the northern part of Los Angeles, adorned with a grand civic centre and a great museum dedicated to the Impressionists, with the statue of The Thinker by Rodin in its elegant gardens.

It was then time to bid goodbye to our lovely, comfortable house which had been our home for ten days. We had a chat with the lady in the house at the entrance who was very nice and gave us a lift to the airport where we rented a car, a lovely Dodge. We had asked for a smaller car, but they did not have any so we ended up with this great car at the same price for our journey, which started with the desert and the most beautiful Death Valley, where the temperature can exceed 40 degrees in summer and where in the past ill equipped people had been walking without enough water and perished, hence its name.

This desert went on for miles and miles with sandy dunes and grey dry mountains as a backdrop, changing colour and becoming all shades of brown as the sun went down – it was most spectacular. We visited a ghost town with mainly ruined buildings from the time of the gold rush, and went for a walk in a canyon.

There was also a huge saltpan, all white and flat, where we could walk on very hard solidified salt. This was an unusual walk in an unusual part of the world situated below sea level that we felt lucky to experience. There were also strata and strata of folded mountainsides, and we were able to watch the sunset over the highest mountain near Death Valley.

These contrasts were quite exquisite and just one of the many unforgettable sights which America is endowed with. America might not be the best country for backpacking, and it often requires a car to take full advantage of its scenery and many towns, but being so huge and so diverse with varied scenery and wilderness areas it certainly is worth discovering time and time again.

You can still find accommodation as you go – and we did, as I had not booked any place after the cottage in Los Angeles – so it was still an adventure. You can certainly get lost, however we did have a GPS which actually made us miss the Sequoia National Park and the highest mountain in California, Mt Whitney. Instead we went via a much more uninteresting route before we actually reached Death Valley. The worst part was missing a very close and beautiful area that Marc would have liked to have seen; we will have to go back one day as we also missed Monument Valley which I really regret to this day.

Our next port of call was totally different as we were heading to Las Vegas and its excesses, but I have to admit the town was very interesting and its hotels and gambling places were out of this world. Some of the casinos mimicked buildings and scenery of various countries, with waterfalls everywhere; there was a mini Eiffel Tower and Statue of Liberty, and huge gambling rooms where we did not gamble one cent but where people were gambling huge sums of money. The actual price of food was much more expensive than Allan remembered from when he had gone to a conference there from San Antonio. I enjoyed the Italian part (Caesar's Palace) which had indoor shopping; a ceiling resembling the blue Italian sky; decorations in the form of fake Roman artefacts and columns; gondolas to make you feel you were in Venice; and ridiculously expensive items in very exclusive shops – quite nice to look at, but I was not tempted by all this jewellery and leather. People were milling everywhere in the cold Las Vegas night, a city strangely situated in the middle of a huge desert.

America seemed quite expensive this time round and Allan felt we should shorten the holiday; he was not so happy with America, which had caused a huge financial crisis which was going to drag down Europe as well later on, all due to the greed of some traders, and we looked at shortening our holiday to my regret. In the meantime, we enjoyed what we had left.

The next day was Allan's birthday and we travelled to Hoover Dam, which was fitting as it was such an amazing feat of engineering and appealed to his scientific mind. We spent the day visiting this remarkable dam before returning to Las Vegas for the evening.

We then took to the road again and stopped at Williams on Route 66 in order to visit the famous Grand Canyon.

The temperature was pretty cool and there was still snow on the ground in the attractive town of Williams, where we were lucky enough to find rather nice accommodation at a decent price. We probably would have had trouble in summer and were well placed to visit the awesome Grand Canyon. When we saw our first glimpse of it, we were simply staggered by the sheer beauty and grandeur of it all. It is quite difficult to explain the feeling of awe at this huge natural canyon going on for miles and miles, with an incredible palette of colours changing with the time of day and play of clouds and sun and snow, and the gigantic walls of impenetrable rock. The views were stupendous, out of this world, and we drove here and there, and there were more fantastic vistas of this incredible phenomenon. It was beyond everything I expected, a sheer beauty that you could not be impervious to; this is certainly one place you have to see in the world.

In this beautiful landscape, we even managed to see an equally beautiful deer pretty close to us who did not seem to mind our presence. In the still present snow, he seemed to emerge straight from Father Christmas's sleigh and its reindeer. What a lovely and noble creature; how man can ever shoot at them is beyond me!

We took close to a hundred photographs of this unforgettable canyon. In a way, that is when trouble started; it was so beautiful that I did not insist on going on to Monument Valley, which was not that far away, which I then regretted not to have insisted on reaching it. Well, we'll have to come back one day to visit this area.

We visited one park too many, and after the Grand Canyon, only a majestic one like the one we missed would have been worth visiting. Instead, we went to Joshua National Park, and this would have been interesting at another time, but right then it seemed like just stone after stone and strange twisted trees and roads which were endless.

We eventually left this interminable park and arrived in Palm Springs where the temperature had become warm again and where cacti were growing so high; this was a desert town at the foot of very high mountains, with many windmills on the hills. The mountains were still snow-capped, despite the temperature below. This was our last stop before San Diego, where we were to finish our American trip. We certainly did not do justice to this beautiful California town but what we saw of it was very interesting, and the sky was a perfect blue.

The city of San Diego was a mixture of old and new, a very attractive place. As I mentioned earlier we hardly had enough time and so only briefly saw some parts, enough to show us what an attractive place this was, away from the zone of earthquakes with a constant and very pleasant temperature.

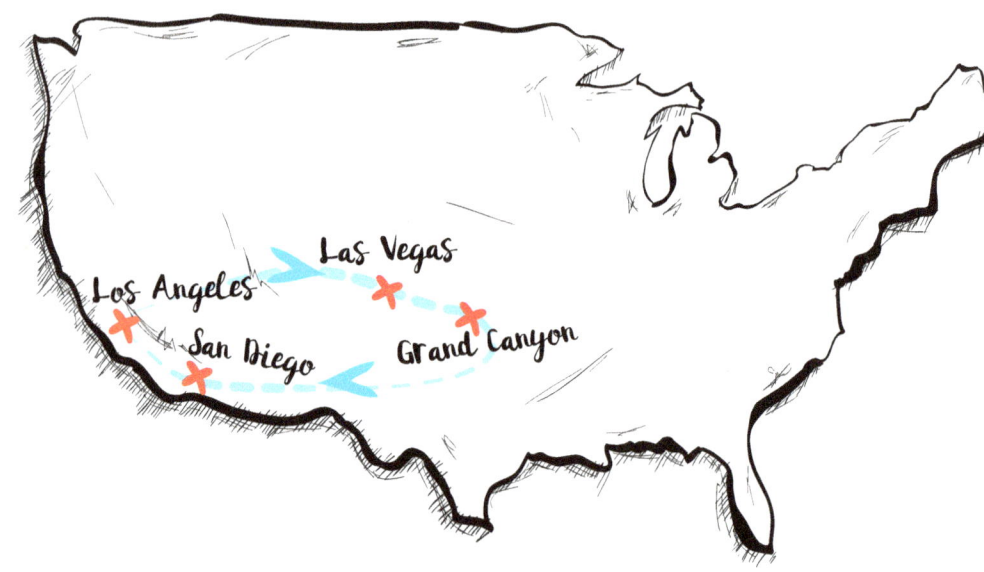

Being situated by the sea meant it had a very important harbour and a naval base; it also had a great zoo and many parks including a park of very attractive old buildings which I meant to visit.

However, as we had decided suddenly that we were going to get back to Australia soon, we did not have time to stay any longer and had to get on the road back to Los Angeles quickly to catch our next flight and say goodbye to our American adventure.

It had been great and it was lovely to experience it with our youngest child, who has been my companion for so long through the various stages of my life so far and who has experienced many a trip with us.

Darwin and the Northern Territory

JULY 2009

Back in Australia, we wanted to go on some trips to discover more of this huge continent and so decided to leave Brisbane at the beginning of the Queensland winter (nowhere as cold as the winters in Europe) to visit the north, and so we took a three hour flight to Darwin, the capital of the Northern Territory. It was definitely tropical country there and pleasantly warm at that time of the year, and probably much hotter and more humid at other times. We visited this pleasant place which had a few colonial buildings that had escaped the terrible earthquake of 1974, which had flattened many buildings and destroyed so many lives. We visited the Parliament inside and out, and strolled down to the picturesque harbour and the fabulous botanical garden with its gorgeous tropical vegetation.

This was one of the few places where we could actually admire the sunset on the sea, as the east of Australia just experiences the sunrise, which has always been too early for us. The sunset was glorious and the beaches pleasant, with a market close by and a lovely promenade by the seafront. There were quite a number of policemen on their rounds there though, and we saw quite a few Aboriginal people hanging about doing nothing much, idly sitting on the floor. This was definitely Aboriginal country and they were much more noticeable than in all the other cities of Australia that we had visited so far.

After having explored what Darwin had to offer, we hired a car; luckily, thanks to Allan, we had decided on taking the best insurance possible. We drove inland and stopped at the Berry Hot Springs, where we could cool down in their lovely warmth before entering Kakadu National Park where we went for a walk in one of the many tracks to discover some Aborigine drawings painted in the many caves around. I am not sure if they were as old as they said, but they were certainly interesting. The scenery around was quite spectacular, with huge rock formations surrounded by many forests. We had a lovely, unhurried day in this beautiful part of the world; the atmosphere was peaceful as there were not many tourists.

There were a few hot springs around and we had to be careful when we did go in the waters of these springs to make sure that this was not crocodile territory; some waterholes were famous for this, and you were not supposed to swim there. There are always some foolish people who will do so however and, of course, some accidents do happen; the Northern Territory authorities seem to know where these places are and you are always warned about them.. It certainly felt odd to think of these prehistoric-like creatures crawling around the place, and I felt a little bit ill at ease whenever we approached waterholes.

The next day, we took a boat on the river where there were indeed some crocodiles in the water and saw some of these scary looking creatures; we were glad we were on board a boat and not walking on the edge of the river. However, the park itself was very beautiful and contained many types of birds as well.

Next we drove further down to Edith Falls and the famous Katherine Gorge. The falls seemed fairly small but the whole area was striking, with huge reddish rocks leading down to the lake, the colours changing with the time of the day, and there were trees and trees galore with nothing to spoil the view; this was the start of the wilderness, and you could imagine what the real Outback would be like further down. It would have been interesting to go down to Alice Springs, but this was still miles and miles further south and we certainly did not have the time to do it, but it is something to do in the future, hopefully. We were quite privileged to be able to visit this northern part of Australia in all its grandeur and took advantage of the opportunity to go walking among the trees in the very well-marked tracks that Australia has plenty of. The temperature was ideal, and it was not the rainy season which affects this area during the entire summer. Again there was hardly anyone else in the vicinity, and we had all this beauty mostly to ourselves.

The next part of our trip was to Katherine Gorge and was going to be the furthest south we would go in order have time to visit another area on the way back up to Darwin. We had another bout of cooling down in yet another hot spring near the gorges; the water was so delicious and for once, it was very reachable for me, and not slippery. I could have spent ages in those warm waters.

But we had to leave as we intended to see the gorges before dark and also go on a long trek up to the top of the gorges. It was quite strenuous at times, but the view from the summit was something to die for, with those huge cliffs and the river snaking along below past some pure white beaches following the contours. There were more tourists here, mostly on boats silently following the river.

Our next port of call was going to be Litchfields where we planned to stop at the place where Crocodile Dundee's Charlie the buffalo had been preserved and stuffed and, coincidentally, where we were going to stay for the night. We drove past some huge termite mounds, and past a kangaroo which was hiding in the woods. Darkness was coming rapidly. We were on a main road with quite a few huge lorries delivering their wares to wherever they were going, and we could see many kangaroos on the roadside. This was not a good sign as it is a known fact that they are not the cleverest of animals, and are attracted by headlights. We were only at five kilometres from our destination when, boom, we hit a huge kangaroo which, sadly, died.

Luckily, the three of us were safe and fine. We got out of the car, saw there was only a relatively small dent where the poor animal must have hit its head, and decided we could drive on as the place where we were staying that night (and which I had booked in advance) was not far away. When we got there we stopped at the petrol station next door to our hotel to phone the rental car agency and leave a message. Then the car would not start, and we left it there and carried our luggage to our hotel. The next day, we phoned the agency again and they sent someone with a trailer who brought us back to Darwin. The driver of the trailer was from East Timor and had been a bodyguard for the ex-president Ramos Hortes, and he was a very interesting man. Luckily we were close to the end of our holiday and did not miss too much,

It was a fair drive back to Darwin and we had one more day to kill, so we just took it easy and spent a bit of time walking along the shore and took advantage of the pool at our hotel. We also had to deal with the not so interesting meeting with the rental car agency, and they were not so happy. The car had just been fixed and was like new and they wanted us to pay a lot to repair it; well, they did not tell us this that day, which is just as well as it would have spoilt our last day in Darwin. But in the following months, they tried to make us pay around $3,000 even though we had bought full insurance cover. Eventually we won – we knew we were right – but it was just as well that we'd had full insurance, as it would otherwise have been a very costly holiday.

We will never forget that encounter with the poor kangaroo, but otherwise we had a nice time.

Rockhampton and the Capricorn Coast

OCTOBER 2009

As there was a long four-day weekend in October and we were still so keen on visiting what was around our area, we decided to push it north to Rockhampton, an eight-hour drive in this vast state that is Queensland. We had decided this was the furthest north we could drive comfortably to do more sightseeing whenever breaks allowed it.

We were not disappointed as Rockhampton was full of grand colonial buildings which were still well preserved, unlike many Australian towns which had sadly destroyed those lovely buildings to make room for modern, bland high-rises. There was a whole street of these buildings, a treat for our eyes, with beautiful white and creamy buildings with those gorgeous wrought iron verandas and elegant columns; stately buildings with round cupolas.

In the evening, we went to a Thai restaurant where I had the most delicious food cooked and presented in a half pineapple, something I have never had since. The next day, we visited a museum with old vintage cars, a school, and all sorts of buildings from the past. Then we reached the Tropic of Capricorn and stood exactly on that line, and for some reason it felt like an achievement. This is the southernmost latitude where the sun can be directly overhead.

The weather was delightful, as it should be in this area, with a perfect blue sky, and we carried on our visit of the aptly named Capricorn Coast, which was quite unspoilt as this was far from the biggest cities of Brisbane or Cairns. So much the better to preserve the beautiful and more pristine nature I had expected to see more of on the Sunshine Coast, which was more built up than I had expected. We took a picture of the entrance to the beach which had a little sandy path surrounded by shrubby hills with wild flowers opening on to the beach and sea like those at Yeppoon on the Emu Heads, giving gorgeous vistas of more beach and sea and hills in the distance, with no buildings to mar the scenery.

There was a cute little harbour with some small boats happily ringing like little bells and adding to the charm of the area. We even managed to see an eagle's nest with the little one in it perched right up the white building, the most graceful 'Singing Ship' (in honour of James Cook) which really was of the purest white standing out against the pure blue sky, with the inky blue shade of the sea in the background.

    This was quite a quick trip to this part of Queensland – it took us a whole day to reach it and a whole day to drive back – but it gave us an impression of the unspoilt coast in this area and was definitely worth the trip, enhancing our appreciation for the beauty of Queensland and allowing our son to discover more of the state he was living in. Again not a backpacking trip as such, as this is almost impossible in Australia where you definitely need a car, but nevertheless a little adventure in the big adventure of life. We wanted to share our travelling adventures with our children as much as possible before they flew the nest one by one, although it seemed we perversely did that ourselves when we decided to go and live in Australia. At that time we left one of our grown up children behind – in hindsight quite a difficult decision which caused some heartache on both sides, but perhaps making us stronger, who knows? Aside from philosophising about life, this was a great and relatively easy trip to undertake.

Vietnam / Cambodia

29TH DECEMBER 2009 TO 17TH JANUARY 2010

As we were now living again on the other side of the world, in Australia, we took the opportunity to head for the closer Southeast Asian countries with the last of our children in tow, who was now able to share more of our backpacking adventures at the grand old age of 16 – and a wonderful travelling companion he was, too.

First, on our quick stopover between flights in Singapore, we gave an *aperçu* of the modern place to Marc – a place that we had seen a couple of times already ourselves. We finally arrived in Hanoi for the start of a two and a half week journey from North to South Vietnam. We – and especially Allan – had always been fascinated by the sad history which Vietnam had to suffer, and we were interested in discovering for ourselves what made these people who they were, besides discovering the country itself. Our son also was very keen on history and going to such places makes history more alive.

Hanoi was celebrating its 1,000 years of existence, quite incredible after the relatively new Australia! We took a tuk-tuk, two of them, actually, which zigzagged through very heavy traffic. It was quite scary at times as we were in front while the men were pedalling behind us and whenever we turned into another street, we were facing fast oncoming traffic consisting of cars and all sorts of other vehicles. They also took us through us the oldest parts of the city with narrow alleys reminiscent of Morocco, and we could smell various aromas of plants and herbs used in cooking.

Later on in the evening, we met up with Allan's potential student who arrived, of course, on her motorbike. Motorbikes in these parts of the world had sadly replaced most of the bicycles which were less noisy but also less quick. We had a lovely dinner with her in a typical Vietnamese restaurant and tasted all sorts of excellent dishes. The following day, we visited the centre of Hanoi and the prison where John McCain (the Republican presidential candidate in 2008) had been incarcerated during the Vietnam War; his prisoner's clothes were still there on display.

Our next destination was to be Halong Bay, famous for its impressive formations jutting here and there all along the coast, and we went on a tour we had booked to be able to spend New Year's Eve on a boat. When we arrived there in a minibus with other tourists, the bay was full of boats bobbing up and down on the calm waters in various states of decoration.

Of course, ours was probably one of the most rickety ones, with layers of peeling paint; our boat had certainly seen better days. Luckily, our bedroom was actually pretty good, and the show of over 2,000 islands was just mesmerising. What a sight indeed: tiny fishermen's villages built right on the water, on rafts even, most likely poor people but with a million dollar view. After playing cards at night with some French people, we went to bed and woke up to this wonderful fjord-like scenery once again. Our son Marc has certainly experienced varied places on New Year's Day.

The following night found us on a train heading for Hué, the old capital of Vietnam, and a taxi took us close to a really good hotel where we stayed for such a cheap price (around 30 dollars); it was a really comfortable and decent place. We did not waste much time and took a nicely decorated dragon boat which delivered us close to the beautiful Thai Hoa Palace, a very colourful site which was still being renovated. Finding a hotel is another great and easy thing to do here without booking ahead, as when you arrive at a station or bus station, you have a few people coming to you and showing you pictures of hotels where they can take you, and invariably they find you very nice places at a very reasonable cost. This is the same with regards to train and bus timetables; the hotels know them and this avoids a long and lengthy trip to the station and gives you more time to get on with tourism. I must admit the system is excellent in Vietnam, and the organisation all around superb. It certainly takes away a lot of frustration; you gain time and money and do not have to carry your bags all over the place. I would definitely advise anyone who wants to travel independently to visit Vietnam. The other good thing about Vietnam was that, whenever we were feeling hungry, there was always a possibility of eating some chicken noodle soup, various breads, and desserts – always at a very decent price. At our hotel that night, the thoughtful owners had left us a cake, and a New Year's card with some coffee and tea offered for free!

The next destination, Hoi An, took us four hours to reached by bus, but the place was a jewel. It is a UNESCO town, again situated along a river, and felt so romantic. We went to a show at the theatre in the evening and there were just the three of us listening to this beautiful, traditional music with the accompanying dances – a lovely show in a lovely place. Marc was at an age where he would remember and certainly could appreciate the beauty of it. We spent an extra day visiting the little streets with ancient and very well maintained pretty, colourful houses in such a delightful setting, and then spent some time at the pretty Cua Dai Beach, four kilometres away, with coconut trees as a backdrop.

There were a few people hassling us to buy some souvenirs but they finally gave up, and in the early evening we had a meal at a little plastic table on the beach like the natives and drank from a coconut, simple and yet paradise-like. Who needs a resort?

The next day, we took a bus tour in order to visit My Son, a historical place which had been bombed by the Americans during the war. In our jeep this was quite atmospheric, and no doubt appealing to my history and war buff companions (husband and son). Then we took a double-decker bus with narrow beds for the next night journey. Geographically, Vietnam is a very long and narrow country and therefore, in order to make good progress, you either need to take the plane or travel at night at times. This was a very interesting experience. I had never seen such a bus before but it was not uncomfortable apart from the bumpy road at times, and a fun way to travel for adults and 'kids'. It took twelve hours, but it did not seem that long; there was definitely much more room than in a plane and you could stretch your weary legs sometimes. Also, the driver was pretty good – it was not his fault if there were some potholes on the road.

Nah Trang was our next destination. People found us a nice beachfront hotel (as they usually do when you arrive at your destination) but it looked too western for our taste after pretty Hoi An. Still, it was fine and we decided to go and visit the Pasteur Institute, but it was closed and instead we visited the beach; it was littered with rubbish and rather disappointing, so we did not stay very long in Nah Trang (which, however, did possess a lovely building in the shape of a lotus).

We were on the road again, this time going inland to Dalat by bus – a nice bus which gave us allocated seats, and free water and wipes, a reminder of the very civilised Turkish ways. We went up and up into the mountains admiring the pretty scenery, and had a delicious meal to reward us after this long journey during which we met another couple with their teenage daughter travelling through Vietnam for five weeks. At that age, a lot of teenagers would rather be with their friends, but both she and Marc did not seem to mind being with their parents. They were not so daft – might as well take advantage when the trips are being paid!

Dalat is famous for having extensive 'flower gardens' which were very interesting, and Dalat is also endowed with a huge lake. Water always featured wherever we went on this trip, and water is always pleasing to the senses. We took a *pedalo* in the shape of a swan and this was very relaxing – at least for me, as I was not pedalling but just letting the others do the hard work, which is another advantage of having an older son stronger than myself.

We later walked to the 'Crazy House', a really weird house based on fairytales with the most unusual shapes you could imagine – quite dreamlike, it would definitely be a place for a very young child, but can be enjoyed by all regardless of age. We met the architect, Mme Dang Viet Nang, who was the daughter of Truong Ching who had succeeded Ho Chi Minh as president. Later on, we visited the rather sad looking summer palace of Bao Dai; it was rather Spartan, considering the last emperor of Vietnam resided there, and very sparsely furnished.

We boarded another bus to travel yet another long distance, about five and a half hours, to Mui Ne. Despite the length of the journey (in a country where you have to cover large distances to see the sights available in this long and thin nation) the transportation was excellent and, as I mentioned earlier, to be able to find a place to stay on arrival was a *jeu d'enfant*. Having said that, we experienced some difficulty finding a hotel this time as many were in the shape of resorts; the beach was hidden behind all these resorts. The Russian 'invasion' was the reason for this phenomenon. We had some western food that evening and that was not a brilliant idea, as Marc actually felt sick and spent the next day in bed. So it was just as well to leave him there with water and some dry biscuits in the freshness of the room while we walked to the beach with its lovely cockle pastel coloured shape delicate fishing boats, apparently like what had been in South Wales in the past. Then we went on an excursion by jeep to Fairy Spring, where we walked in the clear waters of the spring with golden dust shimmering under the sunlight and which we disturbed, dancing like gold crystals beneath our feet. The jeep then took us onto lovely white, creamy, and rusty red sand dunes on which we walked; poor Marc would have loved the dunes. The moral of the story is: sometimes it is best to stick to the local food rather than western food which might not be so well prepared – something worth remembering for both adults and children.

Our next port of call was to be Saigon – as its ex, much more romantic name was – or Ho Chi Minh City, as its new but rather staid modern name is. We found a hotel following a 'guide' through a maze of streets and took a taxi as quickly as possible to make sure we had time to visit the really moving War Remnants Museum. This museum provided an account of the horrors during the Vietnam War, particularly the napalm raids, which caused so much damage to the civilian population – such a resilient people who dared resist the most important might in the world, and won. Three million people lost their life during that war.

Ho Chi Minh City had the flair of European cities, with broad avenues and some lovely buildings such as the Opera House, the cathedral, and the People's Committee Building.

We had to go and see the Reunification Palace, which had been the scene of the Vietcong victory in 1975, with the most famous picture of a tank forcing in its gates. After this came something more cheerful for us all in the form of a puppet show. Vietnam caters for all sorts of tourists of all ages – no one can be bored in such a place.

We then proceeded on to the Mekong Delta on a tour; tours are really cheap there and when time is of the essence, worth taking once in a while. The Mekong River is huge and the little villages which pepper its sides were quiet; the small boats along the green river adorned with bulrushes took us on a lovely trip, far away it seemed from civilisation, with the elegant women wearing their conical hats and white blouses, their demeanour so very dignified.

The last leg of our trip brought us back to taking a plane – an old propeller drum RT 472 plane which was very comfortable, and this was an interesting experience in itself. This time, I had booked the hotel beforehand, while in Vietnam, for two nights in the town of Siam Reap, Cambodia, thinking we might have difficulty finding a place and not having so much time by now. This was a mistake and I would not recommend booking earlier on in Siam Reap unless it is been done through the Internet with a lot of thinking ahead. However, I now know I would not hesitate to just find a place on the spot as we had done so far.

Our hotel was far from the main attraction and the city centre, and rather expensive for Cambodia – a country even poorer than Vietnam – at 70 dollars! Siam Reap's star attraction is the very famous Angkor Wat, a superb place where you need to book yourself a tuk-tuk, as the site is huge. There were prices for the locals and prices for the foreign tourists, quite a leap actually, but something we had experienced many times in Southeast Asia; it is a practice which, to my mind, is both ok and not really fair. We saw some monkeys along the way, and the incredible Ta Prohm, partly covered by huge banyan tree roots – quite a dramatic sight! Nature trying and succeeding in beating Man!

On our last day, we went to visit a museum which I had heard about; it was located 40 minutes away from Siam Reap where Akina, an ex-child soldier, had been forced to lay mines by the Khmer Rouges and where he later changed sides upon seeing the misery caused by the mines. After the Khmer Rouges were gone, he started removing all the unexploded mines, a very dangerous task requiring much bravery. Indeed, Cambodia was still experiencing some violence until 1999, and the museum helps young people who had lost limbs have an education. Akina is quite an inspiring man!

We then went back to Siam Reap, a lovely town along the river which has beautifully preserved hotels and buildings on one side of the river and, in sharp contrast, very poor, derelict houses on the other side. The Cambodian food was delicious and the night markets very picturesque, but you were soon taken back to the stark reality of the place by the amputees begging on the street. Any tourist with a conscience could not help but be moved, they were quite a sight. Something you could not to forget for a long time, as there were no social benefits here.

I would not hesitate to recommend a trip to Vietnam and Cambodia – we only saw one part of Cambodia, and it is probably quite a bit poorer than Vietnam which is not exactly rich, nevertheless it is a great trip for families. It was a very rewarding experience in a country filled with so many resilient people.

China

18TH SEPTEMBER TO 2ND OCTOBER 2011

This trip was more planned than other trips as I was acutely aware that the country was massive, and that my knowledge of the Chinese language was zero though our son – age 17 by then – did learn Chinese for four years and was going to be of great help. So I booked the various flights myself in advance; first, of course, there and back from Australia, and flights within China, and also a night train. I also booked all the accommodation this time, not wanting to waste time looking while there in the country's megacities. Anyway, it was still independent travelling as I was the travel agent I suppose, and I reckoned we saved a third of the price of an organised trip during the worst part of the year; in fact, we went at a fairly good time of the year.

We started with Shanghai, which was a very long flight, and a taxi ride to the hotel; there was some confusion as to the two beds we required, but we were so exhausted that we managed that first night and were changed to a more adequate room the next day. We walked past the French Concession the next morning, and visited the interesting Dr. Sun Yat-sen House; he was one of the founders of the nationalist movement and was a key figure in the Boxer Rebellion and the toppling of the Emperor, and his actions heralded the onset of modern Chinese history and its subsequent embrace of communism. In the park around the corner, people were dancing and doing tai chi; there was more activity than in Brisbane parks for sure, but it was all done in a calm, relaxed manner. We went to the shikumen quarters, some beautifully restored, chic quarters which were ironically the site of the first meeting of the Communist Party with Mao, and then we headed towards the more modern area with the Place du Peuple, the Shanghai Opera, and the museum, which we did not have time to visit unfortunately.

The next day saw us visiting first of all the poorer area of the old Chinese town, which will probably soon be razed and become part of the complex of apartments adjacent to it, but which looked pretty bland. Another Chinatown for the tourists is very well preserved, with beautifully restored temples and buildings alongside graceful ponds and bright red bridges. It started raining when we left and headed for the Bund along the Yangpo River, famous for its 30s buildings on the one side reminiscent of Liverpool in the UK and the very high skyscrapers of the Pudong business area on the other.

After having found (not without problems, surprisingly) a place to eat in the shopping area of Nanjing, we took the boat and walked on the Pudong side, craning our necks to see the heights of those huge buildings which our son Marc liked very much – unlike his mother – but I have to admit I did wonder at their sheer size.

The next day, we took the bullet train from the incredibly huge and modern station – which looked more like an airport – to Hangzhuou. This had been recommended to us but in hindsight, if I had listened to myself instead, I would certainly have gone somewhere else. Still, the experience of taking such a high-speed train from such a station was in itself worth the trip, even more than the actual destination. Hangzhou was actually 300 kilometres away, and yet the trip had only taken an hour. We walked around an endless lake and just could not cover the whole area around it, it was so huge! It again reminded us of the amazing size of places in China.

The following day saw us taking a taxi back to the airport for our next destination, Guilin. Guilin itself was nothing to write home about, so we decided – and rightly so – to head straight away by minibus to Yangshuo, crossing magnificent scenery of mountains that looked like the Glasshouse Mountains back near Brisbane. The view from our hotel was across some of those natural high-rise formations and fantastic shapes which were seen in the movie *Avatar* – no wonder it was filmed around there. We spent the evening walking through the very animated shopping street, a very pretty street indeed.

After a lovely breakfast on the terrace of our hotel admiring these beautiful formations – now even more impressive than the Glasshouse Mountains with the blue sky overhead -- we walked a good twenty minutes to the centre of the town, eagerly looking forward to the day. We took a small bus to Yangdi, the ideal point of departure to go on the river, and from there we took a raft for a couple of hours which took us alongside staggering scenery. We turned a corner of the river and there were so many more amazing, beautiful sights that we did not know where we should look. A picture was taken with Marc and a couple of cormorants at one of the stops. We reluctantly left our raft at Xinping – a very well preserved town dating from 280 AD with very few tourists incredibly – where we found a little café before returning to Yangshuo on a local bus. This place for me was probably one of the highlights of the trip, and I felt quite humbled walking in such old streets where people had walked so many years ago, hardly changed and tended to with care as it should be. Unfortunately, these windows into the past are too often being bulldozed in the name of progress, but as Marc says that is fuelling China's slow and unenviable task of elevating its massive population to a decent standard of living.

Somehow I believe, maybe naively, that there must be other ways to give the Chinese people decent accommodation despite its huge population. The by-products, regrettably, of this 'progress' are huge grey, cold, and straight-lined high-rises in this part of the world, and sadly in many other parts of the world as well. It was good, however, to see that China does not destroy all its old quarters. As I had often noticed in Australia, the smallest places are usually the ones which keep their cache; the old places are not demolished through greed and business or because of a lack of space in an increasingly populated world where land is at a premium.

Next we took yet another internal flight to Xi'an (pronounced She-an) where the famous Terracotta Warriors lure tourists from all over the world. At a bus stop opposite a specific hotel, we were met by a lady (the owner's wife) who Marc was able to practise his Chinese with and who took us to her flat, which I had booked. I was looking forward to seeing my husband's and son's faces as we entered the flat where imitation warriors were to be seen everywhere; very colourful tiles in the bathroom, as the legs of the beds, and whole statues steely looking at us ... We went out, looking for a bank first, which took a while; the sky here was definitely grey, and yet not because bad weather but rather a huge mantel of pollution which would not leave the city. We visited the Bell Tower and walked through the Muslim quarters, which was very busy, but again it was difficult to find a decent place to eat and we ended up in a MacDonald's, which for once I enjoyed. This was to be a repetitive and annoying task in China, not being able to find a nice eating place very easily, so unlike Vietnam where we could find them more or less everywhere.

Although I had mentioned not eating western food on another trip in Southeast Asia – actually in Vietnam –Mac Do is a pretty safe bet everywhere around the globe due to its hygiene and renowned cleanliness; MacDonald's does have very stringent rules in that regard.

We got up among our own Terracotta Warriors and made breakfast with the food our gracious owners had left for us, then took the bus to go and see the real Terracotta warriors, walking first through some little stalls where we ate pomegranate before heading towards the entrance. There were not-so-nice dog skins hanging everywhere but we quickly forgot that when we saw the extent of the site; the warriors dated from over 2,000 years ago, and were an unforgettable sight for us all. Allan was delightfully surprised as he had not realised that I would take him to the Terracotta Warriors, something he had wanted to see.

The next day we went to the Great Pagoda of the Goose, a nice, modern but also quite beautifully done area with some musical water fountains which were quite magical and, again, which would appeal to any child from a very young age to teenager and young adult. Then we had to go back to our hotel to get our luggage and this time head for the train station, crowded with thousands of people, for our next destination; we were taking a night train to Beijing.

Huge streets more like motorways cross the centre of Beijing, at first look a grey city with buildings everywhere. We were met by the parents of an ex-student of Allan's, Huwei. We took a taxi to the area of the hutongs where I had booked our hotel – an older and prettier area more on a human scale; we had some difficulty again with our booking, but luckily they were able to change our room. Then we were left to our own devices for the afternoon and visited Tiananmen Square and the Forbidden City, quite a fascinating site. Tiananmen Square felt quite gloomy and you could sense the terrible acts that had happened there 23 years before and that, incredibly, the Chinese government still deny ever happened. But the Forbidden City was quite a formidable sight, temple after temple stretching one after the other in an endless round of old buildings, and it seemed to show the might of China. You certainly needed more or less the whole day to go round. On leaving it at the end of the day, we were faced with a sad sight of deformed people begging at the exit, something the Chinese government would probably rather tourists did not see.

In the evening, we went with our hosts to a gorgeous restaurant near Baihal Lake where Mrs. Mao used to enjoy walking around. The restaurant was beautifully decorated with gilded gold and the waitresses were dressed in sumptuous, colourful attire. Dishes kept coming around a round table which you could move, dish after dish, certainly a luxury. We did not know how much this meal would have cost us as our hosts paid for this extravaganza, and it made up for all the meals we'd previously had.

The next day was the other highlight of the Chinese trip as we took a train at a very modest cost to the Great Wall of China. We walked for two and a half hours on this amazingly impressive feat of engineering chiselled into the mountains. Both Allan and Marc walked a little bit higher than me, and, it was just fantastic and definitely better than a tour where people are only allowed a short time to walk. We took our time to just wonder and appreciate this incredible achievement of man all those years ago (and which yet still failed in its task of stopping the Mongols) – the Wall went on for miles and miles. We did not manage to catch the train back as we were too late, but caught a bus which drove us fairly quickly back to Beijing.

We then went to another authentic Chinese restaurant with Huwei's parents in the evening (Huwei being Allan's ex student). They were delightful hosts and their English was excellent; she had been an English teacher and he was a businessman.

The next day we took the tube – which was fairly easy to use – to the Summer Palace, a more cheerful place than the Forbidden City had been, and under bright sunshine for a change. We walked through a beautiful gallery path of paintings reminiscent of Italian art up to the Perfume Hill with a view upon mountains and a pagoda on the other side with a view upon the city – a beautiful fresh-looking place to visit where we spent the whole afternoon. It did not surprise me that this place was named the Summer Palace, as it was cheerful and ablaze with light.

Later on, we were to meet Jin, a friend of Marc's from school who was back in China after two years in Australia, and members of his family. We got lost trying to meet them somewhere in the maze of alleys back in the hutongs; all those narrow alleys looked the same at dusk, but eventually we met at the place they had talked to us about. We were quite late and at some point, they had given up on us. Eventually, we found ourselves with Jin, his pretty mother – a businesswoman who owns some hotel, I believe – and her niece around yet another round table. Marc and his friend were our interpreters for the evening. Later on, they took us to the Olympic site and the famous Bird Nest; we were very lucky as these would have been difficult to reach without any vehicle.

Our last day in Beijing was spent going and visiting yet another temple – probably one too many for Allan – the Temple of Heaven. Its blue tiles were shimmering under the blue sky and we did have a nice walk around this round temple. Then, another meal in the evening with Ying and her husband yet again, before a *Kungshi* show we wanted to see. We were a little bit worried about the timing but we experienced some delicious meals with beautifully dressed waitresses and delicious sweet sweet potatoes. The repetition of sweet is not a mistake! Afterwards, the show at the Red Theatre was most impressive; the Chinese are so good at all sorts of shows and this one, I have to say yet again, was a delight for all ages.

The next day, we had to leave China. It had been a great and fascinating trip which gave us an insight into many things and I believe for a young mind such as our son's, a trip not to forget – as well as a great opportunity to practice his Chinese. Our hosts over the last few days came to pick us up and brought us to the airport where they insisted on paying for another small meal before leaving.

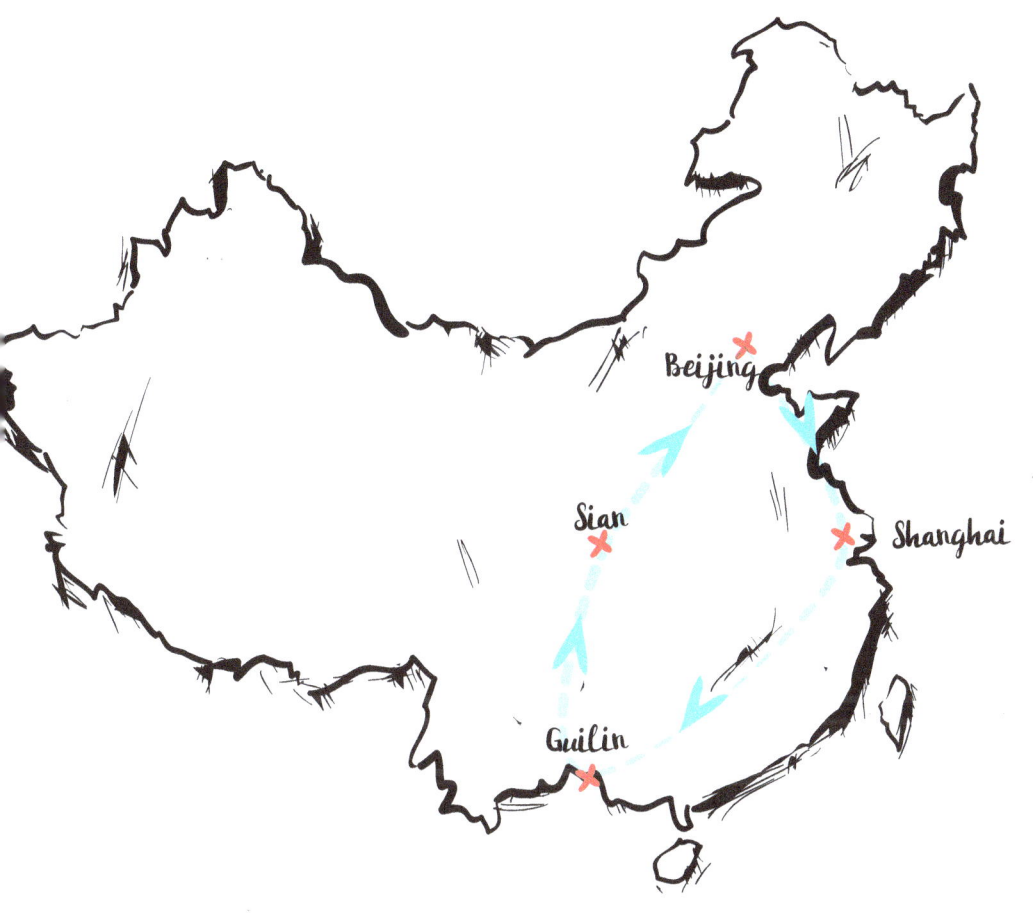

It was with some sadness that we left them, forever grateful for their kindness and attention, and giving us a more personal feel for China.

Here are a few last pictures of the delicious sweet sweet potatoes much enjoyed by all; the great actors in their regalia; and a sign that we saw in Shanghai which said 'Marc' in Chinese (literally meaning Marx, the father of communism). I hope that Marc will renew the Chinese language which has been placed on the backburner since he started university. 📍

Perth and Western Australia

END DECEMBER - JANUARY 2012

As we'd had a big trip in September, we decided to visit more of Australia for one week. Tasmania was a fair contender but the flights were rather expensive whereas the flights to Perth were cheaper, so that decided that, and off we went to Perth. I had booked a bed and breakfast place for the first few nights not so far from the beaches. The place was very pretty and we met a couple of French people staying there who had some family in Perth, but who lived in Paris.

On our first day, we had a lift with another of our co-tenants who dropped us by Cottlesloe Beach, with a famous and quite graceful landmark right on the beach. The sea was pretty cold, surprisingly, considering this was summer and hot and dry – quite a different heat from the more humid Brisbane heat at that time of the year, but apparently not as hot as it could have been as at times it can reach 40 degrees. Later on we walked through the streets of Perth, and saw nothing much apart from the usual high-rises, and here and there some colonial buildings.

There was also an interesting 'English' alley which did indeed remind us of the UK – narrow and quaint with some cheerful Christmas lights hanging above us. From the CBD we went to the picturesque botanical garden overlooking the river, which looked more like a lake. The Perth River was incredibly wide and I guess one of the most interesting features of the city.

The next day saw us in Freemantle on New Year's Eve with its beautiful old buildings. This was definitely reminiscent of an English town in the sun, with its well preserved old churches, its square, and some graceful traditional colonial wrought iron buildings;

It also had a little beach tucked down at the end of the town and an infamous prison which looked quite formidable where many prisoners were held in the past; several had painted some superb murals in their cells. Freemantle must be the prettiest town around Perth; it is very close and somewhere that you could reach via the excellent tramway system which travels through the many seaside towns and numerous suburbs of Perth.

We then celebrated the arrival of the New Year in a little restaurant/café before returning not so late to our bed and breakfast, where we had a lovely breakfast outside in the little yard with the other guests. Our host had been celebrating the New Year on a boat with her husband, which must be quite a nice experience.

We then said goodbye to everyone in this most pleasant bed and breakfast, ready for the next adventure and were lucky to be able to rent the last car from a local company, obtaining it half an hour or so before the place closed. That was a stroke of luck as we could have been stranded in Perth without a car. Our first direction of travel was to the north as I really wanted to see the famous Pinnacles, which were simply fabulous, numerous limestone formations made from seashells broken down ages ago into lime rich sands probably blown inland. It took us three hours to reach this site, first passing many suburbs and then emptiness until we reached it. At some point, Marc was wandering ahead of us and he suddenly came back towards us and explained the reason – showing us a whole family of emus going about their business among the pinnacles. It was quite a lovely sight, but it is best to keep away from these big creatures that could attack and hurt you if they felt their family was threatened. Nevertheless it was a great and unusual photography opportunity to take, and we were very lucky to see these wonderful creatures in such an interesting landscape.

We then returned south, perhaps with some regret as it would have been interesting to go further north, and in fact returned to our B & B for our last night. The distances would have been huge further north and we had decided to go further south instead. We stopped at Bunbury, a little bit disappointing and too touristy for our liking; it was not wild enough, but it was all right. Further south we reached Busselton which has as its highlight a very long 2 km pier. The beaches around were quite inviting but the weather was somewhat cooler; the black and white cormorants by the pier though were a delight.

The further south we went, the colder it became; so much for the hot Perth area. But we still enjoyed our trip and reached Augusta, where the Southern and Indian oceans meet. The coast had become quite spectacular by then with huge rocks and lovely wild flowers sprouting here and there.

We were in Margaret River vineyard country and stopped at some vineyard for a quick wine tasting for Allan, and then visited the beautiful Augusta Caves, the biggest in Australia after the Jenolah Caves near Sydney. Then we were on the road again to go further south to the Valley of Giants; an area of huge trees where we walked on suspended bridges to better appreciate their height – it was great.

We also walked to a tree which seemed to go on indefinitely called Gloucester Tree, which was 60 metres high! We were glad to see different scenery by now and quite happy at discovering this part of this huge country – and we have not finished yet. I think it would take a lifetime to visit it totally, or so it seems.

We aimed to do the whole triangle of the South West region of Western Australia and carried on to pretty Denmark; the attractive town was flanked by a picturesque river on one side and the beach and roaring sea on the other side.

Our last port of call before returning to Perth and Brisbane was the interesting and quite old town of Albury, with many interesting buildings strewn throughout it – as I like – and, of course, Frenchman's Bay where the French had arrived all those years ago; I had to have a photograph there, of course. Many towns in this part of Australia had French names as many had been discovered by the French; for example, Esperance.

The seas in these areas were quite unleashed with some very interesting rock formations such as Natural Bridge and the Gap. The hue of the sea was ranging from deep blue with furious white foam dancing angrily to calm turquoise seas away from the wind. Albany had been the place from which soldiers leaving for Gallipoli had embarked, and a huge Anzac statue was facing the angry sea in their honour. There could also be seen the replica of the Amity boat, which had sailed from Sydney struggling against the elements in the 1820s to form a settlement. Altogether we had a great trip, yet again discovering so much, and it was a pleasure to do so with our son, which enriched our experience.

On the drive back to Perth, we encountered an accident; a big 4-wheel drive had turned on its side with its caravan. It was a strange sight on the other side of the road and with extreme luck the elderly couple was fine, bar some scratches. It shows how you have to be careful even on those long straight roads with hardly any traffic on them.

Kuala Lumpur and Penang, Malaysia

30TH DECEMBER 2012 – 13TH JANUARY 2013

This was going to be quite a different holiday as it was going to mark another time in our lives, a time of change and separation – unfortunately a necessary thing for the time being. This holiday was a sort of fact-finding mission in Kuala Lumpur, to be followed by a week's holiday in Penang. To explain, the end of a job in Brisbane meant another job for Allan in Kuala Lumpur, which he was going to take on starting mid-February, so we had decided to have look at the place and find where to live (well, at least for Allan to start with, or so I thought then). There were to be some turbulent and lonesome times ahead, and so this was not the usual holiday to get away from work and enjoy the trip's dreamlike quality.

We got up very early to drive to the airport at Gold Coast, something I got used to for the next phase of our life. It was just the two of us that left that morning, as Marc was going to join us a bit later. Arriving at Kuala Lumpur, we reached Central Station by bus and took a taxi to the hotel I had booked, strangely placed but with quite a pretty room, albeit quite small. It started raining, and we had some dinner in the adjacent garden sheltered from the rain.

The next day saw us taking a bus to Central Station again to reach the IMU University where Allan was going to work. It looked quite modern and clean inside, looking a bit like a mosque as it had a round shape. Then we took the underground and a taxi to Sri Petaling which was the nearest town to IMU; there were some shops, cafes/restaurants, and bungalows with security gates, but all this was not easily accessible to the university itself. We looked at Cheras on the tube line, but that looked pretty awful and dirty, and then moved on to Bangsar, the expat area which was quite far away, unfortunately. The station there was quite posh and we found a travel agent to see the times of buses/trains to Penang, which was going to be our next destination for a proper holiday.

In the evening we took a monorail to Bintang which was in the more touristy area with fashionable shopping malls, and looked at the Pavilion Mall with beautiful Christmas decorations; it looked quite fairy-like, no expense spared!

We then went to the hotel where we had stayed the last time on the way to a conference in Kerala, and we had a couple of drinks to celebrate the New Year there. We did not know then what we knew now. The whole town was excited with everybody wishing each other happy New Year. There were huge crowds but everyone was in a good, festive mood. Afterwards we took the monorail again before midnight, then had a long walk through Little India; then we took a bus to reach our hotel and a better, bigger bedroom.

The following day was New Year's Day and we had decided to go and visit Putrajaya. After breakfast at Central Station, we headed for the place by a quick train; it was well known for being the Canberra of Malaysia, very Malay indeed with the majority of the population Muslim. There were superb mosques, it had to be said, situated along an artificial lake and some pretty gardens as they had tried to make this place a green space. We went for our lunch in the mall in front of the lake and then visited inside the main mosque, where I had to wear some sort of blue cape covering most of the body and my hair. The guide inside explained about the construction of the mosque with marble from Italy and other materials from Germany, and how the mosque had been built in only two years. He also spoke about social life and seemed quite a moderate Muslim. It was quite a relaxing, more holiday-like day to start the year.

The next day was back to reality and looking for places for the future, so we took the LRT towards Pudu, which was not very nice at all, and we also went to another area with ugly high-rises, lots of noise and pollution, and nowhere to walk.

We went back to Pudu, the site of an old prison, with a lot of slums. Afterwards, we went back to nicer Bangsar but that was not conveniently placed. The next day was much of the same, but we also saw the huge Mid Valley Shopping Mall not far from the hotel where we were staying; this was going to become Allan's local mall. On the 4th, we met Marc in the evening and returned to our Orion Hotel and let him sleep later on the next day, walking to the mall and letting him rest.

Later on, we went to the famous Petronas Towers and had a walk in its gardens where it was nice to see some greenery and be able to listen to birds' noise, followed by a fairly mediocre meal in the mall below the towers. The weather was pretty unpredictable, with a lot of rain. We met two possible students of Allan's later on back in Bangsar, lovely girls who could speak Mandarin, Cantonese, Malay, and English – not bad!

Then it was time to go for our holiday proper and catch the bus from quite a modern bus station to go to Georgetown in Penang; the whole trip only took four hours and Penang greeted us with a nice blue sky for a change. We took a taxi to the city centre but had trouble finding a decent hotel – as I had not noticed that the one I was thinking of smelled of cigarette smoke – so we found a room in Cititel which brought the price down for three nights. I was not feeling too well that night and let Allan and Marc go out for the evening.

The following day was Allan's birthday, and I was feeling normal again after a good night's rest. We walked in the rather pleasant city with its white Victorian buildings much better preserved than in KL, and also visited some more traditional and very gorgeous colourful mansions; here and there we saw some pretty rebuilt little houses, ornate and very cute indeed. We also visited a house where Dr. Sun Yat-sen used to meet his pre-revolutionary acolytes, and sat at the table where he used to sit. After having visited China and his house there, it was very interesting and well explained by the guide.

We got up really late the next day and instead of going to the botanical garden as we had planned, decided to go and visit the temples, the biggest complex of Buddhist temples in all Malaysia. It was quite magnificent and we never expected it to be found in this place, 45 minutes away by bus from the city centre and not in a touristy area at all; the whole complex -- sitting on the hill – was worth visiting. Then it was back to the city centre for a nice dinner at Ecco, a restaurant described in *Lonely Planet*, and we were not disappointed; there was no smoke from cigarettes, and it was not situated right on the edge of the road with all the fumes from cars blowing in either. We then returned to our hotel, walking a long way via the pretty 'Love Lane'; we were quite tired by then, but we'd had a good day.

The next day, we left our hotel to reach Batu Ferringhi in the north of the island and found a homestay, an apartment which was so-so – not dirty but not brilliant either – with two bedrooms and a balcony so highly perched it made me feel quite dizzy. We thought we might as well explore the area and went to the beach opposite the homestay, a long sandy beach with very few people in the sea and many hawkers who suggested that we to go on a boat, etc. We just sat down there on the beach to do some reading; the sky had become greyish with a few drops of rain, and we walked on to the town where we ate in a food court and found ourselves another hotel which was much better, and at a decent price.

We stayed on for a bit in our new hotel, enjoying the pool and resting, and then took a bus to go to the national park. We went for a walk in the jungle, seeing some silver fur monkeys above us and a huge monitor lizard on the beach; he looked quite impressive, and we did not try to get too close to him. We walked to and along the Tree Top, which was superb, and then the walk became harder as we tried to reach Monkey Beach with so many roots on our path, climbing over rocks, catching some lianas here and there, and crossing over tree trunks; the walk took us a good two hours. At Monkey Beach we met a nice young couple from Sheffield who were working for one year in Melbourne and who'd had their camera stolen (which they managed to retrieve) by the monkeys, which were indeed numerous on this aptly named beach. We took the boat back to Tahu Pahang and the bus to Batu Ferringhi after quite an adventurous day.

We did manage to get up earlier the next day for a delicious buffet breakfast, something we had not had for quite a while; there was no need to eat afterwards for quite a few hours. Then we headed for Batu Bahang to Butterfly Farm, with superb butterflies and an excellent guide who explained about the 'chrysalides' and how to catch butterflies without hurting them, how long they lived, etc. I was wearing my butterfly T-shirt which seemed to attract them. There were some very interesting exhibitions as well and altogether it was a very nice place, better than the Tropical Fruit Farm where we went later on that day. The guide there explained about some of the tropical fruits which could hardly be seen, and the best part of it was the 'degustation' at the end, where we helped ourselves twice to all sorts of fruit and fruit juices and left feeling nicely full. We walked back to the entrance admiring some gorgeous mountain scenery all around the place, and found our taxi there. This was to be our last day in Penang and we finished it in style in a nice restaurant which was in the shape of a boat after having spent some time at the hotel swimming pool; the waiters were all dressed in maritime uniforms.

The next morning it was time, after our scrumptious breakfast, to take the communal taxi from the hotel (the hotel was rather reluctant, as we were not supposed to have luggage in this shuttle that we had booked the night before and that we knew was a perk of staying in the hotel) to the bus station in the centre of Georgetown. We were early, so we had a look at the dull shopping mall before catching our bus back to Kuala Lumpur. This bus was not as good as the one we had taken to come here; it was an old rickety one without seat belts and stopped all over the place, taking one hour longer this time. Marc suddenly noticed that we had left our Nintendo DS behind, most probably in the bedroom – oh well, sometimes such things happen. Back at our Orion boutique hotel for one more night before heading for the airport quite early, we met Allan's new boss again, this time with his daughter who was leaving Malaysia and who would be going back to the Gold Coast with us. On the plane, I also met a neighbour from Sri Lanka that I had befriended on the way to the shops back home in Brisbane – what a coincidence!

So came the end of an unusual holiday mixed with some research about Kuala Lumpur, and the start of another unsure future yet again, but quite different this time round. Still, it was nice to have shared it once again with Allan and our youngest son.

Sarawak, Borneo

22ND APRIL 2014 – 27TH APRIL 2014

This time round, I was going to travel to Kuala Lumpur with Marc in order to visit Allan, and take the opportunity to visit more of Southeast Asia (Allan and I had already spent a few days in Java and a week in Sri Lanka, but this would be our family time together) and visit Sarawak.

We took the plane first to Singapore, then Kuala Lumpur where Allan resided and arrived on Saturday evening after an eight hour flight with Singapore Airlines, watching some films. The highlight of these films was one about a French writer going to live in New York as his ex-wife had left him to go and live in New York; a very interesting and quite amusing yet thoughtful film, which reminded me of Jim. We then took another short flight to Kuala Lumpur and a taxi to Allan's place where we had some tea and a quick bite, as we were still hungry. It was good to see Allan again – it seemed as if all this time away from him had not been real, and yet it had been a long three and a half months.

The next day, we went to the cathedral for Easter mass; the place was crowded with mostly Indians and Filipinos I guess, and there were some Black people in the choir singing at the top of their voices. The mass lasted one and a half hours, and outside the rain had started pouring down with lightning, so we had to wait a bit longer inside the cathedral until the rain more or less stopped. We walked and took the Monorail to a Malaysian theatre where Allan had booked us three tickets to see *Jersey Boys* about a musical group called The Four Seasons from the sixties. At first, I could not really appreciate it as I did not have a clue who these people were, but after a while and some songs which I recognised, I enjoyed it thoroughly. This was followed by a restaurant in Bintang that Allan knew very well where we had a big meal. This was a full, unusual day and we much appreciated this surprise show – a lovely way to spend Easter.

The next day when Allan went back to work, Marc and I left late morning to take the LRT and Komuter train to the big Mid Valley Mall that we knew now, looking for clothes for Marc; we managed to find a great pair of jeans and two T-shirts, and a new mobile phone for myself even though I don't like mobile phones very much. We returned to the flat under more pouring rain – it can rain so much and so frequently in Kuala Lumpur; we got a bit wet but arrived back at 5.30 pm, the time I had planned to be back.

I started feeling unwell and had a high temperature. I managed to get myself up to cook some lentils, carrots, and eggs with a readymade soup I had bought as a sauce and went to bed early, feeling quite weak and hoping I would be better the next day.

The day of our departure for Kuching, Sarawak, Allan went to work until 3 pm; we just stayed in that day and I laid on the sofa, feeling sorry for myself, but then perked up. Marianne, our Canadian neighbour from below, popped in; it was nice seeing her again albeit briefly, as Allan arrived and we were to go very soon. We took a taxi to the airport under terrible pouring rain – how the driver could even see the road was amazing – and then we took our flight to Kuching. Luckily, by then it had stopped raining. Arriving at Kuching, we took another taxi to the B&B I had booked and although the building was lovely, the room was pretty basic – especially the bathroom – and it was not well situated either. By a stroke of luck, I had not paid for the reservation yet and I used Allan's phone to call Expedia. We were able to get out without paying anything, and took another taxi to the Grand Margherita Hotel, which was much more centrally located and charged a cheaper rate. We got quite a nice room with just a couple of stains on the carpet, but it was very nice and roomy and very well placed. We hit the bed eventually at about 1 am!

The next day – or should I say some eight hours later – we were up at quite a decent time to have our huge buffet breakfast overlooking the river, and set off visiting the very pretty town of Kuching under a wonderful blue sky for a change after Kuala Lumpur. The riverwalk was really lovely and very clean, and the air was clean too. The buildings were pretty, especially the unusual gilded crown-like city hall and the white tower adjacent to it with the Astana on the other side – a pretty white palace built by and for J. Brookes, the white rajah before Malaysia's freedom; the building was now used by the Governor of Sarawak. We walked to the museum area which was covered with some very picturesque colonial white buildings; the museum was inspired by Normandy-style architecture and contained an example of a traditional longhouse. By the end of our visit, we were quite tired and rested on some benches in the adjacent park.

It is to be noted that Kuching in Malay or Indonesian means 'cat'; the actual symbol of the town is a cat, and we could see several examples of cat statues disseminated around the city even though the origin of the name was not very clear. There was a sense of order in this place. I felt that one could drive here as it was not so hectic and not even that noisy, with very few high-rise buildings and therefore a much more open feel, and a pure blue sky rarely seen in Kuala Lumpur, probably due to the pollution.

We walked back towards the river looking at the shops selling souvenirs, and then had a meal in the court-like building restaurant in the yard, very close to the Tourist Office where I had gathered useful information for the coming days, such as bus timetables. We went on a river cruise in the evening, meeting two young Frenchmen on the boat. They were from the south of France and gave compliments about the place where Marc was likely to go and study; they were really nice, bright people. There was also a young, tall woman on her own on the boat, and later on we saw her eating alone. Allan rightly felt sorry for her and eventually Marc and I went to ask her if she wanted to join us for dessert, but she was going back to her hotel. The unfortunate thing that night was that I had diarrhoea all night, probably due to the food – which was not fresh – and the fact that the restaurant was almost empty and thus not able to get rid of its food as safely as it should have.

The following day, I was fine again and had a frugal breakfast of bread, butter, banana, and tea. We then walked to the bus station and took a bus which only cost us 3 ringgit each, i.e. one dollar, to reach the Semenggoh Orang Utan Sanctuary. Orang utan means 'man of the forest' in Indonesian, a well-deserved name. We reached the park early and waited at the bus stop where we had some cake, fruit, and water until it opened, and walked uphill through the dense vegetation. It was lovely to hear nature and the metallic sounds of the forest around us, like in Taiwan all those years ago. Then we met up with the guide and tourists from all over the world, including many Russians who had come by shuttle from their tourist bus up to the parking lot and could not have been bothered walking up the path – yet this was an experience in itself. The guide gave us instructions as to what to do such as making minimal noise and, if you did see the animals coming your way, to just run for your life. He was not joking, but no orang utan turned up in the morning. Then, through his walkie talkie, he heard that some orang utans had been seen at another feeding station, which we reached quickly through a path in the forest. The guide went to the feeding station with stacks of bananas, and two or three biggish orang utans came down the lianas with incredible agility, considering their size and figure. It was a fabulous show of those semi-wild creatures, and it made me wonder why we would want to destroy their environment.

Some of them gently took food from the guide's hand, and others helped themselves and then ate in all sorts of positions, hanging up and down the lianas. A Mum with her baby was enticed to come down as well, and you could see the tree tops trembling showing their presence. Up and down they went while one just happily stayed on the platform. This was purely magical; they were like trapeze artists doing their show, brownish-orange hairy creatures in their natural habitat – quite a humbling sight!

And then, after about an hour, the king of kings came down in all his majesty – a huge animal whose thick hair was swinging from his arms as he appeared so powerful – Ritchie the patriarch! By then, the guide had left the feeding platform in front of this giant man of the forest. There was not much food left, so the guide told us that we should go quickly as they could come down towards us. We obediently did what he said and left this amazing environment and its bright and agile inhabitants.

We waited by the car park as we had asked to have a van drive us to Annarheis Longhouse, which was situated about 45 minutes away and which I knew did not have any special opening hours. It had started raining and thundering slightly by then, but we had been lucky and it did not last. The mountain scenery around was magnificent, reminding us to a certain extent of the Glasshouse Mountains at times – really gorgeous and so tropical looking and, in fact, the driver told us that we were facing the Borneo Highlands and stopped the van so that Allan could take some pictures.

On the other side was the Indonesian side of Kalimantan Island. We reached the longhouse by 5 pm and started walking on the bamboo floor of this huge complex of houses all linked with each other. This seemed quite well organised, simple but very interesting, and obviously some communal arrangement where my brother Jacques would not have been out of place. We talked to a very interesting and clever man with long white hair who explained some of the political situation, and said that people from mainland Malaysia needed a permit to work in Borneo. He was making musical instruments and also playing them, and was going to the UK at the beginning of July to play somewhere in Essex! There was a room that I did not see as it was closed by then, which contained human skulls. These people used to be head-hunters before Brookes came upon Borneo, and the thought of it was quite scary. These people were autonomous and self-sufficient, and the settlement consisted of some 250 people. This was a lived-in longhouse – not for tourists, although it accommodated them – and there were interesting bridges and steps which required some agility to navigate; the bamboo flooring had to be re-done once a year. We then left after more than an hour as Kuching was over an hour away, and went to eat in a café overlooking the gorgeous riverwalk which I could not tire of personally; there were a lot of people from the west in that restaurant.

As I'd had a funny stomach, I wisely had a bowl of chicken soup with some vegetables, which was ideal for me. We walked back to the flat after yet another full day, and I will never forget the orang utans –and neither will Allan and Marc, I am sure. I was glad I fulfilled that promise to Marc at the very least; this was a trip on which I wanted him to come.

The following day, after our usual buffet – four dishes for Allan (Marc and I could not eat as much) – we took the bus to the Cultural Centre near Damai. The weather was not so nice that day and it had been raining, but eventually it stopped. En route, we crossed some areas which were not as pretty – some suburbs not so tidy, but still with quite luxuriant vegetation – and arrived about an hour later to the centre, which was framed by mountains. This was a sort of living museum which showed the various types of housing of the different area tribes. First we visited the Chinese exhibit (they had been encouraged to come and settle) and Allan tried his hand at the big wheel which would have been used to grind the rice flour. We then moved on to the other exhibits: Ulu, Iban, Biddayu, Malay ... lots of these houses were built on stilts with very high ceilings. Inside were people showing us their various skills: cooking; weaving; men in their 'soldier' attire; the blacksmith making swords whose great-grandfather (while he said grandfather, I doubt it) was a head-hunter and that I could believe – a little bit off-putting. We saw different types of longhouses again, these belonging to the more nomadic tribes of the Penan who would have lived in the dense jungles. It was all very interesting, and this was a great museum showcasing these various tribes; the whole experience was crowned by some ethnic dancing which was excellent, not to mention the Malaysian hymn.

We then quickly went on to see the sea; this was a bit disappointing, only a small arch of golden sand and nothing really to walk along. We decided to take the bus back there and then and talked to a young Swedish woman who was soon going to have some interview back in Sweden; she was a lovely person, and Marc had a good chat with her.

We had another meal at the same place as the day before and another stroll by the pleasant river heading back to the hotel, but we were not serenaded as we had been the night before by a great guitarist. This riverwalk was very pleasant indeed, with a lot of activity in the evening, and you felt very safe. In fact, when we changed hotels, Marc forgot two bags in the taxi including mine which had all our papers, tickets, passports etc., but after a phone call from the reception desk (and I believe possibly even without it) the driver came back to give the bags back to us. We were very impressed by his honesty.

Our last full day in Borneo was going to be spent in Bako National Park, and we had to get up earlier in order to fully appreciate this park. We took the 10 o'clock bus to reach it under a perfect blue sky, and the temperature was delightfully warm. A few backpackers joined our local bus and we drove past some housing estates which did not have the sophistication of Kuching centre, but still all had little gardens in front of the 4 and 5 storey buildings, which allowed the residents to put their clothes out to dry.

We arrived about an hour and 9 ringgit for the three of us later (that would have been three dollars for the three of us; compare this with over six dollars to do one or two stops on the river at Brisbane per person!). We had arrived at the park's entrance, but not the proper park, and there we had to take a boat which was much more expensive (about 120 ringgit in return for half an hour) to get us to the heart of the park. The 'ride' on the boat was, however, superb via mangroves high in the sea and great rock formations, and it was quite easy to get in and out of the boat. The captain was very good, slowing down when there were other boats and then speeding along again. I felt totally safe and really enjoyed the trip.

Arriving at our destination we walked to the headquarters, where we had to enrol. There were a few cabins for people who wanted to stay there, like the two French people we had previously met. Around those cabins there were the lovely proboscis monkeys high on the trees just above us; so close, much closer than we had seen them at Brunei on the boat. They were lovely, looking like little humans with their big noses, and they were not aggressive at all and minded their own business. They were a joy to observe; unfortunately they were becoming a rarity, and there were only about 1,000 left in the wild and only on Borneo Island. We reluctantly left them to go jungle walking on a trail (while it was well indicated, it was a very difficult trail with entangled roots everywhere; it just as well that we did not take the original trail which would have been even longer, and we had to be back for the 4 o'clock boat). There were stones of all sizes as well, and every so often some ladder steps – you certainly did not want to miss one and have a fall and a sprained foot or worse. It was just as well that it was not raining and not slippery, as this would have been disastrous.

Three-quarters of the way through our perilous trip came another type of danger in the shape of a family of macaque monkeys surrounding us. They looked pretty aggressive, and nothing like our lovely proboscis monkeys; they were on the ground on their own territory, in the front and at the back of us. I suggested Allan get a stick to frighten them away, and he hit the tree hard which thankfully frightened them away. One of them had been showing its fangs at Marc who had my bag with a sealed bag of crisps inside, but I guess that they could smell them anyway; they could have attacked, and you were not supposed to look at them in the eye. They could give you rabies if you were bitten by them.

After this adventure to remember forever, we reached the idyllic beach with some relief. There were a couple of Italians with a guide and they were going close to the cliff at the end of the beach, so I was curious to know what there was to see.

In the shade of the cliff was a green snake waiting for its prey – a dangerous snake (but tame compared to Australia's snakes) but as long as you did not get too close, you were fine. The young lady was from Sicily and they lived in Milan with their two year old son.

We took a boat back to the main boat with them, avoiding the long walk back, and were able to see the great rock formations under the velvety blue sky, and then had a drink at the headquarters with the monkeys around – but it was fine there. We chatted with a young Belgian couple who were spending six months in Singapore and travelling as much as possible in Southeast Asia. Then we took the bus back to Kuching where we had a lovely meal in a little restaurant opposite the Hilton: the food was from the local tribes in mid-Borneo. It was unusual, lovely, and cheap, and beautifully presented. We had discovered this place thanks to a couple of Polish people who had told us to come in there as they were about to leave the restaurant. The price of one dinner with soup, some great other dishes, and tea was five dollars! It was a great way to finish our trip in lovely, graceful Kuching before sadly having to say goodbye to Allan in Kuala Lumpur the next day.

Conclusion

These trips were summarized to give an idea of the places we visited alongside the notion of travelling with kids independently – something which is still relatively unusual in many families. Also this serves as a souvenir for ourselves of our travelling with the kids; it is a legacy to our children so that they can preserve these memories of us travelling together, something which I cherish and will forever.

These holidays cover around thirty years of traipsing around unfamiliar places, and not much has changed as far as that way of travelling is concerned. I have noticed a few books written on the subject here and there, but they are very few and far between. Often families will still book a week or a couple of weeks in the same resort year after year, whether they live in the UK or here in Australia, and they do not do much sightseeing outside the odd excursion, and come back home having seen very little of the country they visited nor having met the locals, outside of the bartenders. To my mind, this is a great shame; when you travel miles away from home to more or less be confined to a hotel complex with activities mainly consisting of lazing by the swimming pool or the beach instead of going further out of the comfort zone. All that is gained this way is possibly more sunshine, although this is not even valid for the Australians; we have our own resort here, so why look for the same overseas!

Sure, some people just want to have a rest and are quite happy with this option, leaving their children with some babysitter while they have a nap or go out to dinner. True enough, there are times when you would like to be alone as a couple, but this will come quickly enough and I have been reminded many times in the past how this time when your children are small goes in a flash; I feel that even more so now that our youngest will fly the nest and go on studying in France. I am so glad I took advantage of our children as much as possible. Apart from that, a family holiday should be an unusual and special time when you and your husband have time to be with the family, away from the hustle and bustle of daily routine and the rushed, hectic working life. These are precious moments which will always be magical and remain as wonderful souvenirs when your children grow up. As I said, they do grow up so fast and I will repeat it here: twice when my eldest was a baby and then when my youngest was a baby, I was told to take advantage of this time as it goes so quickly, never to return. The time when they are small is wonderful, and the time shared travelling around unknown places with them has hopefully made the family bond stronger. When you are in a foreign place, either travelling alone or living there, these bonds tend to become stronger as there are no other relatives around and you form a tightly secluded capsule which does, however, open to the outside world.

You change for the better from having visited these countries due to the various experiences you have there, some happy and some sad ones – for example, when you experience poverty firsthand. It makes you appreciate your own life and understand how privileged you are to be able to travel freely, and to be able to afford travelling to faraway places. It sometimes makes you feel guilty about your luck of having been born in the west, with all its comforts, and sense of security and stability. I believe – or like to believe – that it makes your children be more aware not only of the physical world around them, but also the value of their own life and good luck.

Travelling independently is still the best way to thoroughly visit a country, and if you can do it as a couple, there is no reason why you cannot carry on as a family. It just requires more organization and more care. You will probably give your children the same gypsy genes, and it will be interesting to see whether our children will carry on travelling in the same way as they themselves did with their own families. As travelling becomes cheaper it should be more and more accessible to whoever has a sense of adventure in them. Perhaps this might make you more world-conscious and more ready to be tolerant in a world which can be hard, where terrorism and the many conflicts are the biggest threat to travelling nowadays. It is such a wonderful experience to travel with your children in tow that I cannot stress it enough. Once you start travelling this way, you are hooked and your meetings with people in those faraway places will be rewarded. The children will only have made it even more pleasurable by sharing your adventures with you.

I want to thank my loving husband Allan for having made this travelling possible, and I was so lucky that he shared that sense of adventure when sometimes things were not always easy and we had to sleep or travel in some discomfort, and that he trusted me to prepare those trips and agreed to take the children on our adventures. I also want to dedicate this book to our children who have been such good travelling companions and hardly ever complained; they made it possible and during those trips showed wisdom beyond their age many times! I actually feel quite sad to have come to the end of this book, as this represents the end of an era.

www.ingramcontent.com/pod-product-compliance
Lightning Source LLC
Chambersburg PA
CBHW041956080526
44588CB00021B/2763